The Hidden Covenant Revealed

Upjohn Aghaji

PUBLISHED BY INSIGHT PUBLISHING
DOUGLASVILLE, GEORGIA. USA.

Copyright ©2019 Upjohn Aghaji
ISBN 978-0-9989277-4-9 Hidden Covenant
All rights reserved

Insight publishing is dedicated to providing well balanced teaching materials and gospel centered products for the edification of the church. Our scripturally balanced tools and easy to use materials will energize and empower believing churches to evangelize, disciple, minister to the youth and children while edifying the whole family. We prayerfully trust that our books will help you with true biblical discoveries that will help your growth while helping others to grow.

Scripture quotations are from the King James Version of the Bible unless otherwise noted. Scripture quotations identified NKJV are from the New King James Bible Copyright ©1979, 1980, 1982 by Thomas Nelson, Inc. Used by Permission. Scripture quotations identified TLB are from the

Rights for publishing this book in other languages are contracted by Insight publishing.

Table of Contents

Introduction

Considering the relevance of the biblical doctrine of covenant, every Christian should have at the minimum, a basic understanding of what the Bible means by this inescapable term *covenant*. It is a shaping factor in scripture and all biblical and spiritual understanding and application.

Covenant is about relationship. It clarifies expectations and protects and strengthens a specified bond. Right from the beginning in the garden of Eden, God made His expectations known to Adam and Eve. They agreed but later defaulted, and we know the rest of the story. God's expectations are usually defined and if you do not grasp this, you are most certainly going to have a bad or at best a choppy relationship with Him *and with others*. A healthy sense of covenant will help with most, if not all, relationship difficulties we encounter. God made Adam and

Introduction

Eve and immediately communicated His expectations. They agreed but went ahead to do the opposite. This is a basic human flaw we often contend with.

At times we falter because we don't know or understand the expectations, or we outright don't care about the other party's expectations: We want what we want at that moment. But the Lord has given us the most marvelous covenant in Jesus called "The New Covenant," the best of all His covenants yet the most misunderstood of all. He wants us to understand why He did so. This covenant solves all natural and spiritual relationship problems—all of them. *God was simply providing a covenant as a way for those who so desired to enter into a relationship with Him to be aware of the need for commitment to him and to others.* In this book, we will uncover why the almighty and all-sufficient God would want to have a covenant with man in the first place.

Chapter One

What Is Covenant?

Covenants are contracts. So we start by stating that God wants a contract with you. He wants it in the same manner you want a contract in everyday life to protect important relationships. Contracts are a part of everyday life. This is how we take care of everyday business in our personal and professional dealings. Whether verbal or written, we encounter them in our daily pursuits. Some contracts are unilateral, and some are bilateral. Unilateral and bilateral contracts are something many people interact with almost every day while not being aware most of the time. Grasping the different types of agreements in our daily interactions and relationships is helpful. Bilateral agreements are the most common type and most people encounter this kind quite often.

What is Covenant?

Fundamentally, a bilateral contract is an agreement between at least two people or groups. Most business and personal contracts fall into this category. You're entering into this type of agreement every time you make a purchase at a store order a meal at a restaurant, borrow a book from your library or download an app or song to your device. In each circumstance, promises are made and hopefully kept by each party.

On the other hand, **unilateral contracts involve an action undertaken by one person or group alone**. A unilateral contract involves only one person making a promise or agreement. Many think that God has made a unilateral covenant-*contract* with humanity and as such, we expect Him to do everything while we have few or no obligations on our part. Contracts are usually binding and serious, so it obviously becomes important that we understand them in the light of God's dealings with us. Webster's dictionary defines covenant as "a usually *formal, solemn and binding agreement*: compact; a written agreement or *promise* usually under seal between two or more parties, especially *for the performance of some action*." From this point onward, remember

What is Covenant?

that you can substitute the word covenant for agreement or contract.

In scripture however, the word used in the Old Testament for covenant is the Hebrew word, "beriyt," which means "to cut" like cutting a covenant, treaty, alliance or agreement. *The English word "contract" still remains the closest in meaning to the Hebrew word for covenant. It simply is a contract but a very different and special kind of contract with specific respect to God's interest with humanity.* In God's human project, the covenants that He deals with regarding mankind are covenants of relationship—special relationships.

Covenants were usually made for several reasons in old times, for example, to bring two enemies back together as friends, or sometimes between families, nations and rulers of different realms. The solemnity of such agreements underscores the need to abide by its contents to avoid serious consequences. Violation of covenant could lead to war and or death, depending on the scope. All written covenants possess similar structures with a section where obligations to the

What is Covenant?

other and expectations are listed. Sometimes they will include a section listing how they would benefit the other. For instance, business contracts are for the mutual benefit of all parties involved and the same is true for peace treaties. The fact is that all covenants have to do with a relationship of one kind or another.

Consider the family unit as a covenant relationship. Whether spoken or unspoken, family is expected to have some kind of fidelity and trust. Individuals are expected to rely on one another. Family usually starts from a couple promising to be faithful and loving for "better or for worse." No matter the wording, the expectation is usually unambiguous.

Friendship is a covenant relationship also. Barring the sex part, friendship and marriage are the same. The spoken and sometimes unspoken commitment with friends is like a marriage. "for better or for worse." In friendship, the same unshakeable idea of "be there for me through thick and thin," is undeniably present even when it is not voiced out. In fact, this is the basis of marriage. It's the same, "I will be there for you no

What is Covenant?

matter what." This is what we all yearn for. Hence, of all of these, the closest reflection of God's covenant with man is the marriage covenant. It is possibly the best way to gain the more proper perspective regarding this subject.

Obviously, God values and needs to protect His relationship with us because He loves us but we have the tendency to look for other gods to replace Him. That was the point of the great commandment of, "Thou shalt love the Lord thy God with all thy heart, and with all thy soul, and with all thy strength, and with all thy mind; and thy neighbor as thyself," mentioned in Luke 10:27. He started by telling us that we shall not have other gods because we have that tendency. God values His relationship with us, but He also wants something out of this whole deal. He in turn wants to be valued by us. Surprised? Similarly, in marriage, your spouse wants something out of it also. Keep that in mind.

Many people rush into marriage thinking of what the spouse will bring to the table, but what about what you will bring to the table? The same selfish attitude extended to a spouse is extended to God as if He wants nothing from you. Again, this kind of covenant relationship that God has prepared for those who so desire, can be exemplified within the marriage relationship. In fact, God does so many times in the Old Testament scriptures by calling Israel His "betrothed," His "wife," and even "adulteress" when they went "whoring" after other gods, and by naming Himself as her "husband." The Church is called the "Bride of Christ" and Paul says he "espoused" us to Christ as our "husband." I find it revealing.

The marriage relationship is based upon certain basic things, (whether spoken, or unspoken but expected) *promises and obligations*, and *unconditional love.* That's all the Father wants from us...unconditional voluntary love. This is the meaning of "Thou shalt love". He wants us to promise to love because then we cannot claim He didn't state what He wanted. The marriage relationship starts with "Thou shalt love" also but is legally binding and can be violated and nullified by acts of infidelity or unfaithfulness. Likewise, unfaithfulness to the Lord is not a recommended behavior. Please, hear these

What is Covenant?

words and take heed. Jesus said that;

"everyone who acknowledges me before men, I also will acknowledge before my Father who is in heaven, but whoever denies me before men, I also will deny before my Father who is in heaven", (Matthew 10:32-33 English Standard Version, ESV).

While Paul admonishes Timothy that;

"if we endure, we will also reign with him; if we deny him, he also will deny us; if we are faithless, he remains faithful" (2 Timothy 2:12-13, New International Version, NIV).

Chapter Two

Covenant vs Testament

Somewhere in the beginning of most Bibles is written in bold letters the words, Old Testament, and right before the book of Matthew is written New Testament. This word testament has made it a little hazy in the mind of some regarding the actual intent of God to establish covenant relationship with His people. As we know, the words testament and covenant have been used interchangeably over many years. I may do the same at times in this writing for easy reading; although, the two words are not totally the same. To clarify, a covenant is an agreement between two parties still living, as in a marriage covenant, while a testament pertains more to the distribution of property and possible benefits after one's death, as in, "last will and testament." The word testament is from the Latin testamentum. Also, the translators considered the Hebrew *b'rit* and the Greek *diatheke* to be the

Covenant vs Testament

equivalent of the Latin testamentum.

Howbeit, the Hebrew word *b'rit* has the general sense of an agreement. Therefore, since the first major division of the Bible focuses on stories recorded during the period of the covenant made at Sinai between God and the people of Israel, it has to accurately be referred to as the Old Covenant. However, *diatheke* can means both "testament" and "covenant," depending on the context, but in most cases, *diatheke* should be translated as "covenant." However, there are a few instances where it can be understood in context as "testament." For example, in the case of a will, it is necessary to prove the death of the one who made it, because a will is in force only when somebody has died; it never takes effect while the one who made it is living." Hebrews 9:16-17 NIV

In this instance, the writer tells us that Christ remembered us in His will. He left us an invaluable spiritual legacy: forgiveness of our sins, the removal of all guilt and the promise of eternal life. All of incalculable spiritual value. These are all part of the New Covenant contract

Covenant vs Testament

Jesus presented, but only became available after His death. His *"blood of the covenant that was poured out for the forgiveness of sins"* made salvation possible for many. Note that a covenant is not the will; although, the will can be found contained in the covenant. Thus, the pages in the bible, famously known as the New Testament scriptures, are simply a record of both a covenant and a testament. The more accurate term should be New Covenant. Therefore, a more correct way of marking the two main divisions of the bible would be the Old Covenant Records of the Patriarchs and Moses and the New Covenant teachings and records and Testament of Jesus Christ.

Finally, worthy of note is the fact that by necessity, God had to implement two main covenants in order for the plan of redemption to succeed. The Mosaic Covenant (also called the Old Covenant) is the first of the two, and the second is the New Covenant. We will focus on the New Covenant for the purposes of this writing.

Chapter Three

Before I Agree

"For which of you, intending to build a tower, sitteth not down first, and counteth the cost, whether he have sufficient to finish it? Lest haply, after he hath laid the foundation, and is not able to finish it, all that behold it begin to mock him, Saying, This man began to build, and was not able to finish.   So likewise, whosoever he be of you that forsaketh not all that he hath, he cannot be my disciple." Luke 14:28-33 ESV

I am about to join a gym and I have had the usual consultations with the salesperson. I chose the membership package I was interested in, then came the conclusion; a document was generated on the computer for me to sign. It seemed too long to capture only the brief discussion we just had, so I resolved to read through it. The salesperson seemed impatient, or at best, surprised that I was taking time to read through it. She said, "Just sign here and initial there, it's just a standard contract." So, after briefly and scantily reviewing this document, I signed it. It was clear that most people would not read through the whole thing and she was ready to be done with the process. Many of us have been in similar situations on different occasions. We encounter covenants every day when we move into an apartment, buy into a subdivision or an estate. We are presented with it on minor transactions like signing up for iTunes, downloading a new app on our phone. Whenever you sign an agreement, you have entered into a covenant which, in some instances, if you do not read the agreements properly and simply scroll down to the "Agree" button, you may have signed up for more than you bargained for. Many of us may find that we actually gave an unknown entity unfettered access to our computer information, phone contacts and photos.

God's covenants present the same opportunity for clarity and understanding, The New Covenant is more serious than an iTunes download or making a transaction in a store, getting your product and checking out. It helps to read, pause and think and "count the cost" before we enter into agreements with God or anyone. (Luke 14:28-30). But we are often so focused on what we want at the moment, we simply click the "Agree" button or sign on the dotted line while mentally deferring the possible consequences for a later date. We just want the product right now.

Many individuals come to the Lord in times of desperation. There may have been a bad diagnosis from the doctor, or persisting financial and or personal problems. We need an immediate solution. We will agree to anything and we make promises that we don't know if we really mean. We just need relief from our troubles by God…a miracle, an intervention at all costs. We promise to love Him, serve Him and make any profession necessary to get relief from the Lord.   Worse is that this seems to be "the gospel" for many preachers.

Preachers are often guilty of telling the crowd to "receive the Lord Jesus," followed usually by a list of things they will receive from Him, with no indication that the Lord Jesus might want something from us or want us for some purpose of His. So then, when the Lord starts making demands and giving instructions, we are startled and surprised. We almost act as if Jesus never said, "count the cost," or "deny yourself," or "pick up your cross." (Matthew 16:24)

When He expects us to wake up in the night and pray for someone or extend ourselves to the unloved, we start making excuses. When we are persecuted for His name's sake, some are totally taken aback as if we did not know this was part of the deal... and many actually did not. When our lives are in mortal danger for identifying with Him, some may want to change sides and turn back.

As a matter of fact, many did not know what they were signing up for because they were simply told about Jesus the problem solver, and God the provider or Jehovah the healer. While all these are real benefits of walking with the Lord, they were not turning to God in real heart felt repentance. It was not mentioned that repentance from selfishly distancing themselves from their maker and taking God's love for granted was required. Someone told them that it was all about them and their needs and fulfilment. How can God have a need? Why would God want anything from

The New Covenant

us? But He does. He absolutely does and deserves whatever He desires from us because He made us.

He doesn't just want something from us, *He wants us*, all of us, our whole being. He wants us back, He wants our love and worship because He made us for Himself.

"for thou hast created all things, and for thy pleasure they are and were created." Revelation 4:11, KJV

We are therefore, His building according to 1 Peter 2:5, His "spiritual dwelling place," His real estate, and your body is "His temple." To deny Him is to deny Him His rightful possession, His property, which amounts to spiritual fraud because you are not your own (1 Corinthians 16:19-20) in the first place.   We were lost and dead and He found and raised us. We owe Him our lives.

Yes, God loves us and will give the world to us, but that is not the point of salvation. Like I have already mentioned, the truth is that we were created for Him... for His pleasure. Not for your pleasure but His. We were lost and He retrieved us from the clutches of sin and death. He salvaged us from the trash dump of rebellion and sin. We find our pleasure in pleasing Him. View it in this manner; God is love and made us out of love. It is safe to say that love needs someone to love or else love is not being expressed. So God (who is Love personified) made us for His pleasure (to be objects of His love) as stated in 1 John 4:9, "In this the love of God was manifested toward us, that God has sent His only begotten Son into the world, that we might live through Him," because Love has to love (be expressed) and be loved (1 John 4:19) (to complete the circle) for love to be fulfilled. In other words, God needs to love and He fulfils His need by creating people that He will love, and they will love Him back which is also our need.

See? this is not that complex. He simply wants to be the object of our love and affection. And He deserves it. After all, "he first loved us." He now wants us to voluntarily love Him back because true love is always voluntary. Covenant simply means we know, understand, agree and are willing to do this. We are therefore. saying to God that we promise to love and cherish Him in return. We cannot claim to be like Him if we are not full of love because God is love and we are made in His image...the image of love. This explains why He enters into covenant with man. He wants us to present our bodies to him as taught by Paul;

"I beseech you therefore, brethren, by the mercies of God, that ye present your bodies a living sacrifice, holy, acceptable unto God, which is your reasonable service." Romans 12:1

He wants to dwell in us and with us like anyone wants to spend time with the one or ones He loves. Yes, He wants spiritual closeness. This is not weird.   Not at all. It's like a marriage, in essence (Ephesians 5:22, 23). You want faithfulness from your spouse, friends and family, right? Okay. You are like Him!   You also want to spend a lot of time with the ones you love?... You truly are made in His image if you need loyalty from the ones you love. He loves spending time with His people. Your time is very valuable and who and what you spend it on will show how dear that person or thing is to you. It is impossible to claim to truly love God and not spend a lot of time with Him. Show me your schedule and I can tell you where your heart is.

He made it easy for us by loving us first and all we need do is to respond. **We read;**

"And we have known and believed the love that God hath to us. God is love; and he that dwelleth in love dwelleth in God, and God in him" (1 John 4:16).

and

"We love him, because he first loved us" (1 John 4:19).

God has shown His love by sending Jesus to give us life. The word says that we live through Him, that is the closeness He requires, *Him in us and we in Him*. The oneness enjoyed in heaven has been extended to earth. Jesus said in John 17 "that they may be one as we are one." So, "we in Him and He in us" reflecting Him.

Again, our greatest need is to love and be

loved. To reject Him is to render yourself useless and worthless, one who should be thrown away—thrown into *hell* to be burned in the refuse dump. But He chooses to redeem us and accept us in the beloved (Ephesians 1:6). Marvelous to consider. A person who does not love is a useless person to God. Listen carefully, it will always be about God's love for us, but that's because He is love and requires…who knows? Billions or maybe trillions of people to love and express Himself through. This is profound. I am serious when I say deny God access to your spirit, body and your life is straight up theft and fraud; it is theft by conversion and ought to be punished.

"You are not your own," 1 Corinthians 6:19.

You are God's property and always will be. You were made for Him. You will never be your own you will always be His for eternity. This is a good thing.

When you enter into covenant with God, you promise to return to Him what belongs to Him in the first place, for you did not make yourself. He did. Will you promise to love, cherish and obey

The New Covenant

Him? Will you promise total devotion even to the point of death? Will you promise to love Him for better and for worse. The great thing is that you will never lose in the end. He has prophetically shown us in His word how it all ends in eternal bliss. You have no excuse anymore. When you spend your limited time here living for Him, He will give you endless time called eternity- with Him.

Loving the Lord and serving Him will come with challenges in this hostile world, but the other option is to be separated from Him. Please consider Christ's words, in Luke 14, verses 27 and 28 (New King James Version, NKJV),

"And whosoever does not bear his cross, and come after Me, cannot be My disciple. For which of you, intending to build a tower, sits not down first, and *counts the cost*, whether he have sufficient to finish it?"

Ask yourself if you are willing to go all the way with the Lord.

The word "cost" mentioned in the previous

paragraph was not introduced by me in this conversation. Cost, amount, payment, outlay, disbursement, these are all related words. Jesus actually spoke that word cost and went on to explain the consequences of not doing so. The result is embarrassment. Folks, God wants you to count the cost of following Him! He does not want you embarrassed. But you can't count the cost if you don't know there is a cost. There *is no cost* to you for salvation because someone else paid for it, but you should still count and consider what it cost Jesus to save you. But *there is* a cost to be His disciple, to identify with Him and to follow Him to the end. It will cost you your life, your plans and more. Your life must become His. He gave you everything and wants everything from you. *Everything,* folks.

It was Jesus' teaching that you should engage your mind and know what you are getting into. While you are at it, you must count the cost of *not* following Him. You must accept that you will enter through the strait way (hard way) not the easy way (Luke 13:24). You must agree that "to live is Christ and to die is gain" (Philippians 1:21). You must be willing to accept that your own family could possibly reject you for your beliefs (Matthew 10:34-38; 19:29; Mark 10:29).

You must also be willing to accept that ultimately, as Christ stated, "...you shall be *hated of all nations* [emphasis added] for My name's sake" (Matthew 24:9). You must accept that "if they persecuted him, they will persecute you." You must "Present your body"—all of it, not some of it. You must be willing to lose your life to gain it, you must be willing to give all you have to the poor if called upon to do so. You must love your enemies and be willing to sell all to follow Christ. If you are a Christian, you agreed to obey. Did you not? You agreed to make Him your only God. Did you not? You agreed to shun sin. Did you not? Hopefully you were told that you were agreeing to such terms. Here's the problem.

A lot depends on how the gospel is presented to the world. The prosperity "everything will be fine" gospel did not help at all. Actually, it has been a demonically-charged teaching sent by the devil himself to destroy the people that God made. The church is still plagued in one form or the other by this underlying mindset. Salvation does not cost you anything spiritually or materially or financially but following Christ? It does cost you everything.

So again, you must present your body a living sacrifice. Your whole body and nothing less (Romans 12:2). Your life must glorify God, your sufferings must glorify God, your progress must glorify God, even your death must glorify God (1 Corinthians 6:20).

Thanks be to God that He is a good God! We can be grateful that He is gracious and loving to us, but still He requires that our mind is present in relating to Him. There is nothing wrong with coming to God during a time of desperation. Indeed, that is when many of us turned to Him, as we saw the depths of our own need. But once we have come to Him, we must learn to walk in the knowledge of His requirements. This is the covenant we have made with God Almighty. The new covenant provides the grace needed to translate us into His family and by an act of faith elevates our position to heavenly realms. No matter the cost, it is worth it to follow Him because you are following Him to eternal bliss.

The New Covenant

There is no cost of following him that is too much. Even if you lose a leg, an arm or your life, you have still made the best choice. Jesus died for our sins and has become our way back to our heavenly Father. We confess Him as Lord and believe that He rose from the dead and we will be saved. Jesus did not suffer on the cross so that you will be a millionaire. He is the lamb that takes away the sin of the world. He is simply inviting us to eternal habitations with Him. He wants us to get it down in our soul when He said;

"... if your eye causes you to sin, tear it out and throw it away. It is better for you to enter life with one eye than with two eyes to be thrown into the hell of fire." (Matthew 18:9 ESV.

So, there you have it. One eye, no eyes, one leg, no legs etc. whatever the cost, it is worth it. Just make it in with Him and you will never suffer again. Confess the Lord Jesus and believe that God raised Him from the dead and you will be saved. Call on Him and He will answer you.

Chapter Four

The New Covenant

**"In speaking of the New Covenant,
he makes the first one obsolete.
And what is becoming obsolete
and growing old is ready to vanish
away."** Hebrews 8:13, ESV

"Old," "obsolete," and "vanish" are the words used by scripture to describe the old covenant. These are strong words and should be taken seriously by every believer. Should we not avoid towing along something that has been declared by God to be "done with" and "obsolete"? It is of importance to identify the "old covenant" and discard it quickly while totally embracing the new. Because

"He taketh away the first, that he may establish the second" (Hebrews 10:9).

The New Covenant

Scripture is stating clearly that the old covenant is finished and irrelevant to our existence right now. Jesus is not playing around as some may think. He suffered, shed His blood and died on the cross to establish this new covenant with His own blood. In fact, His blood is also known as;

"the blood of the covenant" (Hebrews 9:20, Matthew 26:28).

Jesus would not give his life for something that is not of extreme value. In this case there is eternal value and eternal consequence involved.

If we think of the new covenant as books in the bible, we then become unsure of what to do with Hebrews 8:13 where we are clearly told that the old covenant is obsolete. So, the lingering question is usually this: "Do we not read from Genesis to Malachi anymore?" The answer is that we should absolutely read the whole bible, but remember that the covenant we live by today is in our hearts and understood with our minds. In other words, it makes sense when properly understood. This covenant is the most vibrant and dynamic agreement in the history of man.

The New Covenant

"This is the covenant I will establish with the people of Israel *after that time*," declares the Lord. "I will put my laws in their minds and write them on their hearts." (Hebrews 8:10)

The New Testament actually began two thousand years ago. Yes, *"after that time"*; the time of the old. The new covenant relationship became available to us when Jesus our Savior shed His blood on the cross. Your new covenant relationship with God begins when you accept Christ's sacrifice for you, inviting Him into your life. When you sign a marriage certificate, you don't carry the paper with you every where you go but you carry the commitment in your heart. The life you live as a couple starts "after that time" of being single. When you get married, your life is no longer yours and your body is no longer yours in a real way. Same with this covenant.

The Most Serious Covenant

If this is not important to you, it is important to the one who gave His life for you and shed His blood to establish the covenant. One must not underestimate what God will do to those who take the blood and this covenant for granted. Now read these words from the apostle to the Hebrews and subsequently to us,

"He that despised Moses' law died without mercy under two or three witnesses: Of <u>how much sorer punishment, suppose ye, shall he be thought worthy, who hath trodden underfoot the Son of God</u>, and *hath counted the blood of the covenant,* wherewith he was sanctified, an unholy thing, and <u>hath done despite unto the Spirit of grace?</u> For we know him that hath said, <u>Vengeance</u> belongeth unto me, I will <u>recompense</u>, saith the Lord. And again, The Lord shall judge his people. It is a fearful thing to fall into the hands of the living God" (Hebrews 10:28-31). [Emphasis added]

If Moses' law was despised, the consequence was capital punishment. What do you think will happen to the one that despises the New Covenant? Answer: sorer punishment and recompense. That is exactly when to expect vengeance from the Lord and you don't want that because it is fearful, dreadful, horrendous, terrible and awful thing to be in God's eternal bad books. When the New Covenant is despised and rejected, the result is not favorable at all. Therefore, the new covenant is not just some books in the bible to be read, but a bona fide agreement between God and man that started 2000 years ago and is extended to whomever wishes to come into it now. It is a contract He signed with the blood of Jesus. It is that serious. The Lord will judge you if you have;

"...done despite unto the Spirit of grace"

How to live our lives under this new economy called the new covenant is priority. I encourage you to set aside some preconceived ideas and pay attention to the word of God without bias. Listen, the moment you confess Jesus as Lord when you make the decision to follow Christ, you have entered into a new covenant-contract with God and with others in the family of God. You are then expected to walk in this new revelation.

John puts it this way;

The New Covenant

"Whosoever shall confess that Jesus is the Son of God, God dwelleth in him, and he in God" (1 John 4:15).

The Greek word confess here **Homologeo**: ὁμολογέω: *hom-ol-og-eh'-o*: Is from a compound of the base of **G3674** and G3056 in Strong's Concordance meaning to *assent, to **covenant**, to acknowledge:-* **con-(pro-) fess**, confession is made, give thanks, **promise**.

Please notice the words, "covenant" and "promise." You have agreed with the fact that Jesus is Lord. You have entered into a covenant and you have promised to submit to Him as your Lord! You have pledged to give Him yourself without reservation the same way He is giving us Himself without reservation. To be saved means also to be saved from the mindset that made you think that your life was your own. I will state again that if you do not return yourself to the Lord, you become useless and deserve to be discarded in the refuse dump of unusable lives. It is not God's wish, but everyone cleans house at some point. He is not willing that anyone should perish. But many are satisfied with perishing

The New Covenant

Covenants are about defining and protecting relationships and relationships are what we are made for and from. A relationship is usually a "two-way street." He does not covenant with people so that He can be held accountable, but the reverse is the case. He needs to hold you accountable. You are the one who may default and not Him. He covenants with us so that He can have us to Himself. Remember that we were made by Him and for Him, not the other way around.

Christianity for most has been presented as a way to qualify for God's help and blessings, usually measured materially and otherwise. Church is usually for most, about what they can "receive" from the Lord and the church. Things like teaching, healing, counseling, financial breakthrough, good marriage and in some cases, especially in the African context, sometimes a way to get pregnant and have children. I am not kidding.

While all these are possible and reasonable to expect, it is all selfish and still all about you. That's the problem right there. I am serving you notice now that God wants something too. Yes,

The New Covenant

we read the whole bible but we must not return
to the old.

Chapter Five

The New Covenant Is About Commitment

"And when the hour came, he reclined at table, and the apostles with him. And he said to them, "I have earnestly desired to eat this Passover with you before I suffer. For I tell you I will not eat it until it is fulfilled in the kingdom of God." And he took a cup, and when he had given thanks he said, "Take this, and divide it among yourselves. *For I tell you that from now on I will not drink of the fruit of the vine until the kingdom of God comes.*" Luke 22;14-18

Jesus shares a covenant meal with His followers and reminds them that He is committed to meeting up with them in heaven. He literally assures them that he will not celebrate or drink wine or have any covenant meal unless they all unite in the kingdom. This is where holy communion comes from and this is what it is all about- commitment to God and to one another. For more on this subject, read my book "Holy Communion: What Every Christian Should Know".

However, many years ago, I was called to a pastoral ministry in Africa. I was eager to teach the believers what the Lord had been showing me regarding commitment. This was exciting because everyone wants commitment from their friends, loved ones and acquaintances, right? It was easy to see that Christians should lead the way in this matter being that our whole faith is built on trusting the Lord and the Lord trusting us as we trust one another...right?

I had written out some words of commitment on paper based on scripture and thought it would be nice for all of us to read them and agree together and possibly sign them. It included words like "I will not lie to you," "I will not talk negatively about you behind your back," "I will seek your good and progress before mine at all times," and a few more. But to my total surprise, no one said these words willingly and certainly no one signed the paper. Instead they accused me of being an extremist, insisting that I was "taking things too far."

They also cited that there was no biblical precedence for that and certainly no need. But in fact, the need is glaring, and it was all based upon scripture. Yes, based on the same scriptures we all profess to believe, such as Philippians 2:3-4 (NIV);

"...in humility value others above yourselves not looking to your own interests but each of you to the interests of the others."

In other words, prefer your brethren and be honest with the Christian family. Then there's Ephesians 4:25 New Living Translation (NLT),

"So stop telling lies. Let us tell our neighbors the truth, for we are all parts of the same body."

Are these not the "stuff" Christianity is made of? Of course, they are and there are many more to consider. How many times have you been disappointed by so called Christians? How many times have we used words like brother, sister,

The New Covenant

family or friend with no serious consideration about commitment? These are all covenant words that carry a lot of weight. There is need to say them honesty.

We should be able to look one another in the eye and declare these sorts of biblical agreements to fully understand the expected level of purity of our fellowship with one another. In reality we agreed to all these when we became believers. There should be no hesitation in a Christian saying to another one that they won't lie to them. Unless of course you intend to do so.

They neither said nor signed the paper on which these words were written. Needless to say, the church was plagued with the usual scourge of pseudo brotherhood and pretend sisterhood. Lack of closeness and relational apathy took over the group. After a while we started a home fellowship in Georgia and repeated the same suggestion and got the same results. Truth is that the average Christian is not trying to commit to anyone as such, although they want commitment from everyone else. Some want commitment from the church when in need of counselling, financial assistance, etc. Most want loyalty from pastors and leaders without being committed themselves. How does that work? Some want others to check on their well being while they check on no one.

Church is simply people committed to living their lives together in community, fleshing out the life of Jesus. The word must become flesh and be lived out. John 1:14 states that;

"the Word became flesh and dwelt among us, and we have seen his glory, glory as of the only Son from the Father, full of grace and truth."

Likewise, we become that;

"...known and read by all men" (1 Corinthians 3:2).

All of us together are read by all men. It is not just you as an individual because this letter was written to a church. We the Church together relate in an expression of the word of God in our hearts. The way we relate to one another is an expression of the word we study and believe in... our actions thereby are known and read by all men. People read us and sometimes don't like what they read. They instead should be drawn to the Lord and his community by what they observe. In a sense, the church is an "open book," whether we understand it or not.

Is this why Jesus prayed that all believers should be one? The same exact word that is used about marriage "the two become one." (Mark 10:8). New Testament standard beckons us to rise to the point where everyone hurts when one part of the body is hurt. That is a high but sound biblical standard. I am concerned that we have lowered the standard and the enemy wants to come in like a flood. We will see a church without spot or wrinkle when we pay attention to these words. There are practical steps we can take to this end. I have included some suggestions for group discussions:

Create groups within your fellowship. Ask these questions and write down the answers. Why am I afraid of commitment? Am I willing to overcome this? Am I willing to discuss how I feel with others?

Possible reasons for commitment phobia:

- Disappointed by leadership

The New Covenant

- Betrayed by people in the past

- My commitment was taken for granted

- I have been ostracized because of a difference in opinion

- Approached inappropriately by the opposite sex or taken advantage of

Pray together in this manner:

Lord Jesus, please tear down all walls of division between us and help us to forgive every transgression so we can become one. Expose every falsehood and create a real and spiritual bond among us again. Let your love bind us together and help us express your life towards one another. Expose and remove those that contradict your plans and direction for your people.

This discussion does not have to be limited to your local fellowship, approach other believers in similar communities. People will not be committed if they don't want to. But if they never agreed to anything, they can always claim they did not know. If we do not lovingly confront this elephant in our church room, we will continue to remain distant and disconnected. We may preach love and never see the closeness intended by God for His people. Without this it becomes easy for us to walk away from one another for with the flimsiest of excuses. Allow this to be the new chapter in our Christian walk as the body of Christ.

Chapter Six

Brother Jenkins Leaves the Church

Brother Jenkins, stopped coming regularly to weekly fellowship. He was offended about something and wanted to register his offence by withdrawing himself from the communion of the saints. Not surprising to many, such behavior is routinely used to register grievances and brandished as a weapon to "punish" the ones who have "offended" us. This is wrong and should never be so. Commitment demands that "things are discussed" among brethren. We are required by Jesus to "tell our brother" when they wrong us (Matthew 18:15). I am not sure we understand that God is not interested in our fake worship when there is discord. I am not sure we believe that our worship is fake when discord and offence is not addressed.

Brother Jenkins Leaves the Church

When we join a group or local church we have agreed or covenanted with those individuals to meet at a certain time, serve in a specific ministry, to become one. We build relationships and grow together. We have committed to have one another's back. We become used to seeing one another and supporting one another spiritually, emotionally and financially. Therefore, when it's time to leave, we should articulate to other members the reasons why, especially when an offense is involved. It gives others an opportunity to change their ways if they are doing wrong and we must forgive and move on. It also is a growth opportunity for all involved. The one leaving might even change their mind after seeing that the problem may not be with everyone else. It is almost cowardly to simply leave without notice or dialogue. At the minimum it is childish and runs counter to the cause of Christ.

When brother Jenkins left, no one knew why he and his family did and it affected the morale of the group. No one could tell why and the tension was real. Should he think about others and not just himself? When asked to explain to the group the reason why such decision was made, he responded that he only makes decisions for he and his family. So then, the rest of the group were never seen as his family as far as they were concerned. Was there any real bond in the first place? Majority of Christians do not recognize other believers as actual and real family. This is not sound thinking at all. It takes time and work to build relationships and we must take it seriously. When we break fellowship and move on with minimum regard for the others' feelings, we help to create the atmosphere of extreme caution and apprehension in the body of Christ. With the emanating lack of trust, it becomes increasingly difficult for people in the group to "open up" to the next person. This makes connecting even harder. The biblical concept of community becomes a casualty.

Church is not just a place we go to but a community of believers that share their lives together... at least that's what it *should* be. We simply don't "stop going" because we are offended about something. We at least try to work things out because your sudden unexplained withdrawal may discourage someone. Your talents and gifts will be missed therefore creating

Brother Jenkins Leaves the Church

a void. Sadly, most people view church as a place they go to and leave without being questioned. This is evidenced by the term "where I go to church." The thinking is that I go to this church to learn and not necessarily to connect with the others who attend. This implies that when I get fed up for whatever flimsy reason, I "will stop attending, "I will go somewhere else." Many dear saints make it a point to remain distant and unconnected for easy detachment whenever desired. Is this the church that Jesus gave His life for?

Church is not a place. I cannot repeat this enough. Church is people. The ecclesia (called out ones). We are together, the church. No one person is the church. Your body might be the temple of the Holy Spirit, but it is not the church. No one person is the church; it is not possible. No one person is a family, although that individual must be present to create a family. Much like how a tree is not a forest, although there is no forest without the tree. Our connectedness is what makes us unique from the world. Our *inter*dependence not *independence* is what God is interested in. Interdependent commitment is how we become

Brother Jenkins Leaves the Church

the city on that hill spoken of in Matthew 5:14-16,

> "Ye are the light of the world. A city that is set on an hill cannot be hid. Neither do men light a candle, and put it under a bushel, but on a candlestick; and it giveth light unto all that are in the house. Let your light so shine before men, that they may see your good works, and glorify your Father which is in heaven."

You are not the *individual* on a hill but the *city*. Many pastors and church leaders have been hurt so many times that they try not to be connected to the ones they minister to. They also prepare for the day when one will leave. Our survival depends on unity and this is a direct function of commitment, I cannot emphasize this enough. This explains why no one ever really has all they need or want at all times, but together every need is met within the body. We will all need someone sometime if for no other reason than to listen to us and or offer emotional or morale support. We must examine our conduct toward one another or we will continue to have many different church meetings in one building and another two hundred churches on one street. It is not minor but a major departure from biblical standards. We remove ourselves from marriages, we remove ourselves from friendships, and from business contracts just because we are offended over minor and insignificant reasons. We give up on relationships easily; this apathy is observed by the larger society and they lose respect for us.

We should never use withdrawal of fellowship as a way to make a point because withdrawal of fellowship is a last resort and the worst-case scenario. This is no joke. There is injury and pain involved, heartache and negative health consequences involved when relationships sour. It is not something to be used to punish a friend, a spouse or a pastor and church members. It is reserved for fornicators and the covetous. (See 1 Corinthians 6). It is used for the most extreme circumstances.

My friends it is okay, yes, even scriptural to consider the other person's feelings even if they have hurt you. God uses separation as the worst eternal punishment. Separation from Him is akin to spiritual capital punishment. Is this not what God did to Jesus on the cross? It clearly was the only pain that made Jesus cry and the only time he cried out in pain. The beatings didn't make him cry, the nails, the thorns not even the spear made him cry, but God denied him fellowship for a moment and Jesus felt forsaken. Indeed, if we do not feel the pain of separation, then we were never connected. If it does not bother you when there is discord and there is distance, then you must check your heart and ask yourself what is going on inside.

Again, the new covenant is about commitment to one another and commitment to God. Nothing more, nothing less. A commitment to love and cherish God as He has loved us and to love and cherish one another... *"love God and love your neighbor as yourselves"* in simple terms (Matthew 22:37-39). It is this covenant of love for one another and for the Lord that reflects the nature of God. It is also this type of biblical Christianity that is missing today. I am praying that this writing will spur you to consider your relationship with the Father and with other believers. The world is waiting for you and the

Brother Jenkins Leaves the Church

church is waiting for you, people of intense commitment and closeness to one another and the Lord. This is the manifestation of the true sons of God. Individuals who deeply care for, have love for one another and are honest with one another. Not given to shallow lip service but willing to respond in love and commitment.

The end of all things on this side of eternity is near and the Spirit of God is calling us to truth and honest Christian brotherhood. We must be real, and according to 1 Peter 4:7-11 in The Message Bible;

"Everything in the world is about to be wrapped up, so take nothing for granted. Stay wide-awake in prayer. Most of all, love each other as if your life depended on it." [Emphasis added]

Other versions say "fervently," "deeply" and so on. The new covenant has elevated our relationship with the Father and one another. The new covenant has created a family superior to the natural family. The new covenant seeks to lift humanity back to the higher spiritual beckoning of our Father God. This is clear from Jesus' definition of his family. He simplifies it when He said that;

"whoever does the will of God, he is my brother and sister and mother" (Mark 3:35 ESV).

He obviously was not particularly impressed with natural familial ties. He did not think it was the ultimate relationship as we do. Spiritual family was everything to Him and we should follow His example!

When God made Adam and Eve, they had family challenges although they should have been the best match. Eve came from Adam's rib; not the next village or next town but from himself. Yet they had differences and their children had differences to the point of murder. Natural family is over rated. The spiritual family is the real family, although hard to embrace by the carnal mind. It is true nonetheless. Don't mind the fake Christians, we are real family. We must get it right, and we will in Jesus' name. The end is near and the love of many are growing cold and satan is unleashing the final assault on our faithfulness to God and to one another. The day you called yourself a Christian is the same day you covenanted with the millions of other Christians to become one family and one blood by the blood of Jesus Christ our Lord.

God's covenant relationship offers faithfulness, unconditional love and care; it offers a true and stronger, spiritually-strengthened familial relationship through Christ, in addition to acceptance and the promised spiritually-charged affection that can heal hurts and the deepest scars. In a way, the Christian covenant relationship is a "super" relationship; stronger and more versatile than any basic natural ties. The covenant relationship combines the best aspects of all individual natural relationships, creating a supernatural family bond of great power and worth for all parties involved. This super relationship is exactly the kind of unbreakable link that God wants to have with His people. The spiritual family builds a spiritual city superior to any city known to man. And this city is set on a hill as an example and a beacon of hope and refuge for a struggling world.

Brother Jenkins Leaves the Church

We all have the basic "Creator-Creation" relationship *to* God, but eternal life is found only within the context of a relationship *with* God through Jesus. There is a very big difference! Fellowship with Jesus and other believers is non-negotiable, especially when there is no sin. Again, we should never terminate fellowship at will and for childish reasons. Childish reasons are usually selfish reasons. The people of God will need to pay attention to the scriptures and focus in on the real business of relationship-building not brick-and-mortar building, a.k.a. church building or conveniently masked as "church growth." We must stop feeding the beast; the unique danger posed by the obsession over big and expensive buildings is that it merely feeds the leader's ego and does nothing more than suck the life out of the true church community. It enjoys the misplaced energy that should have gone elsewhere to more spiritually energizing pursuits. It keeps humanity from viewing the church in her splendor—the real church.

This terrible mindset seems to have taken the people of God captive. Most Christians have fallen victim to this shallow understanding of church.

Brother Jenkins Leaves the Church

Many years ago, I was invited to a fellowship on a celebration day. The hoopla was in celebration of the multi-million-dollar building they had just paid off. I will tell you about that day: The place was charged with excitement and jubilation as the members were thanking God for this accomplishment. The "pastor" boldly declared that "the church had been paid off." Unfortunately, the church was the building since most of these individuals may have still owed money on their own homes, cars and who knows what else.

I truly was amazed at the level of naïve celebration by individuals who had paid off a multi-million dollar facility while they owed on cars and homes and other big-ticket items. Some of them were outright broke and lived on food stamps. They had been hoodwinked and did not even know it. They did it for God, or so they thought. The building is usually referred to as the house of God. What God? Our God, the Most High? No. He does not live in temples made with hands. No matter how big and expensive it may be.

"Church people" are still among the poorest

Brother Jenkins Leaves the Church

in the world even after years of hearing a prosperity message. By contrast the early church enjoyed such a positive environment. The Holy Spirit was moving powerfully because they understood community and invested in people instead of buildings. The immediate world took note as they were drawn to this community. Their numbers were growing, and people sold property to make sure others were okay. Imagine it right now. Land, homes, etc., were sold not because they wanted to "prosper" or because they were sowing a seed expecting God to do some miracle or the other. This was a miracle! The fact that there was so much love and commitment was a legitimate miracle and for this reason, no one lacked.

> **"There was not a needy person among them, for as many as were owners of lands or houses sold them and brought the proceeds of what was sold and laid it at the apostles feet and it was distributed to each as any had need."** (Acts 4:34-35 ESV).

Brother Jenkins Leaves the Church

Did you get that? *There was not a needy person among them.* That is real church model laid out by the Holy Spirit and approved by the Father. Anything less is questionable. When covenant is real, everyone is taken care of. But then, Ananias and his wife Sapphira broke covenant, broke commitment, broke trust and started "playing games." God killed them. Yes, He did; read it again, the church starts with God killing fakers. Not the devil, but God removed them immediately. Does God value trust and commitment? You tell me. Some say that God does not do such anymore, but think again. The reason God is not physically killing such folks today is because many truly do not know the "gospel" truth. However, no one can deny that His hand of judgement has been upon the church, considering the kind of leaders we have been *punished* with for years now. Many will not make it to eternal habitations with the Lord for this reason.

Will you rise up and do the right thing? Will you have a change of heart? Will you take this covenant-contract seriously?

Recently, some churches have provided

Brother Jenkins Leaves the Church

written church membership covenants to be signed by prospective members. Some agree with this concept while some disagree. The thing we all can agree on is that this move proves that we are recognizing that lack of commitment is a plague now. What will you do or what shall we do? We must ask the Spirit of God to fill us with the love of God daily so that we will overflow and touch all those around us. The call is to love fervently like Jesus loves us. To go beyond loving our neighbor as ourselves and to love fellow believers the way He loves us. To put our lives on the line for one another. John puts it this way;

"Hereby perceive we the love of God, because he laid down his life for us: and we ought to lay down our lives for the brethren" (1 John 3:16). Selah.

Chapter Seven

Just Do It—You Have His Spirit

"For if you live according to the flesh you will die, but if by the Spirit <u>you</u> put to death the deeds of the body, you will live." Romans 8:13

You can and you should defeat the flesh and overcome sinful tendencies. The New covenant has armed us in a way never known to man. We have been given a new spiritual impulsion. We have been given power over our flesh finally.

"*...For God has done what the law, weakened by the flesh, could not do*. By sending his own Son in the likeness of sinful flesh and for sin, he condemned sin in the flesh, in order that the righteous requirement of the law might be fulfilled in us, <u>who walk not according to the flesh but according to the Spirit</u>" (Romans 8:2-4 ESV).

Just Do It – You Have His Spirit

The difference between the old and the new is that *"God has done what the law, weakened by the flesh, could not do."* Therefore, you can live by the Spirit, a life that is not controlled by sin. God has freed us from sin but also empowered us to overcome sinful tendencies. The new covenant is liberating because God has put His Spirit in us. Because He lives in us in a real way. He lives through us and expresses Himself through us. We are now able to do all that God wants us to do. But that is only if we live by the Spirit. Paul continues to say, **"But if Christ is in you, although the body is dead because of sin, the Spirit is life because of righteousness;**

"If the Spirit of him who raised Jesus from the dead dwells in you, he who raised Christ Jesus from the dead will also *give life to your mortal bodies* through his Spirit who dwells in you" [emphasis added] (Romans 8:10-11, ESV).

The Spirit of God gives life to your body. Did you get that?... ***to your body!***

Just Do It – You Have His Spirit

Your body, your flesh cannot overcome your spirit anymore because God has given life to it by the Holy Spirit.   Your spirit will dominate and tell your flesh what to do, not the other way. But your mind must be set on the things of the Spirit because that's where life is. You can love your neighbor as yourself now, we can be honest with one another, we can put our brothers first and we can flee fornication and renounce greed. We can avoid debauchery and evil concupiscence. All that the word said we could do becomes possible now. Just do it and watch it become part of your life and become as simple as breathing. Just do it, forgive and be merciful, be courteous and be affectionate and reliable…just do it…you can now be obedient, honest and trustworthy.

Jesus showed us that it all is possible by the life He lived. He left us an example that we must follow with the help of the Holy Spirit of God. The old covenant through the law could not accomplish this because the Spirit of God was not yet given to all who would ask. Jesus had not yet come to make this special delivery. His spiritual enablement to live like He did. Your body, your flesh, your emotions and lusts cannot overcome you anymore. You are free now in every sense of it. That is the new covenant in action supercharged by the blood of Christ spiritually flowing in your veins. Receive and trust, love and commit in Jesus' name.

It is literarily the Spirit who keeps your mind on the things of the Spirit. It is He who gives you the spiritual hunger required and the thirst for righteousness. It is He who removes your mind from the fleshly and carnal focus. It is He who reminds you to read, study and pray. He nudges us to evangelize and intercede. He removes your mind from materialism to more spiritual values. He saves us from the impending disaster that is the final product of carnality. We would be heading to spiritual and physical death otherwise. God has done a great and marvelous thing.

So, we read in Romans 8:5-8 (ESV);

"For those who live according to the flesh set their minds on the things of the flesh, but those who live according to the Spirit set their minds on the things of the Spirit. [emphasis added] **For to set the mind on the flesh is death,**

but to set the mind on the Spirit is life and peace. For the mind that is set on the flesh is hostile to God, for it does not submit to God's law; indeed, it cannot. Those who are in the flesh cannot please God."

Now we can please God. Now we can resist and overcome sin, now we can obey God and serve and be dedicated to Him and one another. We just need to do it. Just do it. We can live according to the spirit. We can totally submit to God. Yes, we can.

The Law was given and it became an indictment against humanity. It was given because man was not able to walk in righteousness. What does the new covenant do? It gives man the power to live under *the Law of the Spirit of life in Christ Jesus* (Romans 8:2)—to walk in righteousness before God. I believe this is the very essence of the New Covenant. What the Law could not do, the new covenant does: It empowers us to obey God. The new covenant carries with it the power to break sin's hold upon our lives. Hallelujah! I will emphasize this scripture again.

Just Do It – You Have His Spirit

"For **what the law could not do**, in that it was weak through the flesh, God sending his own Son in the likeness of sinful flesh, and for sin, condemned sin in the flesh: that the righteousness of the law might be fulfilled in us, **who walk not after the flesh, but after the Spirit**" *(Romans 8:3-4).*

The entire Law and the Prophets sought to teach man to walk in righteousness before God. But they had to rely on man's power to do so. And that never really worked for very long. But the new covenant is different: It allows God's presence to dwell in us. It brings a true transformation in us, so that the bondage we once knew falls away in the light of God's presence in us.

Is that all there is to it? God just wants us to stop sinning and be obedient, so He doesn't have to put up with our wrongdoing? Not at all! The reason He desires that we walk in holiness before Him is so that we might be in continual communion with Him and others. He wants us to know Him, to walk with Him. His desire is that sin would no longer be allowed to cut us off from our fellowship with Him and other brethren. The law came with curses and near-impossible barriers to overcome, given the weakened state of the unspiritual man. God is Spirit and real fellowship with Him is only by the Spirit.

Paul wrote that;

"Christ hath redeemed us from the curse of the law, being made a curse for us: for it is written, Cursed is every one that hangeth on a tree: That the blessing of Abraham might come on the Gentiles through Jesus Christ; that we might receive the promise of the Spirit through faith"(Galatians 3:13-14).

This text in Galatians is crucial. It cuts right to the heart of the matter. First, we find that the only way to enter into this covenantal relationship with God is through Christ Jesus. There is no other way! "Christ hath redeemed us." There is no one else. There is no other place of safe harbor, no other means of salvation, no other way to come into covenant. None, save Jesus alone. It is He to whom we must run, He to whom we must bow, pouring out our hearts before Him. It is to Jesus that we must cry out with all our hearts, seeking His forgiveness and restoration. Only Jesus.

Second, we see that the blessing of Abraham also comes through Jesus, for it is His Blood which has ratified the covenant. Now we need to notice that the word speaks of "the blessing." This is not a mistake of translation. The word is singular. Throughout the Old Testament accounts, we read of the pursuit of blessing. However, the new covenant would make the true blessing available to humanity. But, it also brought with it a new realm of responsibility. That blessing is the Holy Spirit. The promised blessing is the Spirit of God. The scripture clearly states, "we might receive **the promise of the Spirit.**" Jesus blesses us with Himself—His Spirit. How incredible is that? The spirit of God makes true fellowship possible. The apostle John wrote that;

"We proclaim to you what we have seen and heard, so that you also may have fellowship with us. And our fellowship is with the Father and with his Son, Jesus Christ."

Just Do It – You Have His Spirit

1John1:3

The Holy Spirit is the game changer. The availability of His Spirit to all. That is the power in this dispensation. God's laws are now internalized. He has taken up residence by His Spirit in us. He continues through us to reach out to complete His work of salvation and reconciliation. We surrender to His will and give up our bodies as His temple. We are owned completely by our Lord. It is no longer what we want, but what He wants from us that determines our course of action in life. We completely identify with Him until the world no longer recognizes us. The secular world will treat us like Jesus if truly you identify with Him and conform to His life. If that is not the case, you must ask yourself why. Seek to find areas of compromise and you will find them. Jesus said clearly that,

"If the world hate you, ye know that it hated me before it hated you. If ye were of the world, the world would love his own: but because ye are not of the world, but I have chosen you out of the world, therefore the world hateth you.

Just Do It – You Have His Spirit

Remember the word that I said unto you, The servant is not greater than his lord. <u>If they have persecuted me, they will also persecute you</u>; if they have kept my saying, they will keep yours also" (John 15:18-20).

Just do the right things. You can live right and allow His light to shine. You may not be applauded and it is not always easy, but it is always right, and He smiles upon us. Remember that we are crucified with Christ. They see *Him* now and not us! We are citizens of a different country, strangers and pilgrims in this present world. This new contract requires us *not* to love the world or the things in it. We must recalibrate our worldly engagement. The apostle writes,

"<u>Love not the world, neither the things that are in the world.</u> If any man love the world, the love of the Father is not in him. For all that is in the world, the lust of the flesh, and the lust of the eyes, and the pride of life, is not of the Father, but is of the world. And the world passeth away, and the lust thereof: but

Just Do It – You Have His Spirit

he that *doeth* the will of God abideth for ever" (1 John 2:15-17).

Did you notice he that "doeth" the will of God? It is not he that "knoweth" the will of God that abideth forever but he that "doeth". Again, just do His will with the help of His Spirit. Friends, we can do this by His grace. Let's try today to be honest with one another, let us stop using and abusing one another. We can do business together without defrauding one another. We can build each other up and not tear our brothers and sisters down. We don't have to be in competition with one another anymore but seek our brothers' and sisters' good and progress. We can do this. Yes, we can. Say, "I can do this by His spirit who is my helper." Amen. The Lord's desire is to deliver us from the world, while we often want to take the world with us! This creates confusion in our minds as we try to hold on to the very thing that holds us back. We will cease to be those people who can only see as far as their own misery, fear and need. How different this is from the one who understands that it is his need for the Lord that is the root of his present distress—no matter what your life's circumstances look like at the moment, the Lord is the one you really need. The Lord and your neighbor should be the focus of your love and not the world and the things in it.

Please understand the contract and realize that being born again is the beginning of a new life of genuine responsibility. When we accept Jesus as Lord, we should know that God does not delight in empty words. He expects us to be people of integrity. He wants us to be people who say what we mean, and mean what we say. He doesn't want us to come running to Him only when we're in some sort of trouble, expecting Him to bail us out again and again with no commitment to Him and to others.

Unfortunately, much of today's theology is a needs-based, humanistic teaching that points us toward a heavenly Santa. He stands ever near, ready to grant our wishes and desires whenever we do him the favor of asking him for something. Or we may have been taught that God loves us and places no demands upon us. After all, it could damage our self-esteem if we were ever to hear that He might possibly be displeased with us. This is foolishness!

Just Do It – You Have His Spirit

Now, God will heal you of your illness, provide for you and protect you. But are these the most important things? Certainly, the healing of your physical illness is important to God. But it is not as important as the healing of your spiritual sickness, for the physical will pass away, while the spiritual is eternal.

Is God concerned with the physical as well as the spiritual? Certainly. Does He heal physically as well as spiritually? Of course. But He also looks to what is eternal, not just to the temporal. Of what gain is the healing of the physical body if the spirit is still lost in sin?

We need to adjust our thinking so that we begin to see as God sees. Let's allow Him to renew us and to transform us. The truth is that we were and are bankrupt, no matter how much of this world's goods we have, unless we have Jesus. Without Him, without His indwelling presence, we are still wretched and sick, and quite frankly, dead. Wake up, read the book, understand the contract/covenant, agree with God and go ahead to do His will. It is in this that you will find freedom and eternal reward.

Just Do It – You Have His Spirit

Some may be skeptical of the new covenant at first but that does not mean they are chronic doubters. The gospel requires understanding to be efficacious. Jesus said that;

"when anyone hears the message about the kingdom and does not understand it, the evil one comes and snatches away what was sown in their heart" (Matthew 13:19 NIV).

He continued to state clearly that there is also;

"someone who hears the word and at once receives it with joy. But since they have no root, they last only a short time. When trouble or persecution comes because of the word, they quickly fall away" (Matthew 13:21 NIV).

You see, it is in your best interest to understand what you are agreeing to, the covenants you enter into and most of all, the covenant you have entered into with God. Let us not be lazy as the people of God, but search the scriptures to see what the Lord is desiring and requiring of us. Let us seek to enter into the blessing He has prepared for us. Let us also be responsible enough to tell mankind the whole truth of God's word and His expectations. Just do it.

Chapter Eight

It is Finished

"For this is my [Christ Jesus'] blood of the new testament [or, covenant] which is shed for many for the remission of sins." (Matthew 26:28)

Listen, my friends, sin has been dealt a lethal blow. If anyone says that God sent His Son to die for your car, stop them from such childishness. Jesus did not need to suffer and die on the cross for your house, cars and other things. He did not hang on that cross bleeding for any material thing. God had been giving people all kinds of material possessions before Jesus came.

Sin was the problem and the problem is solved in Christ. He taketh away the sin of the world, He does not cover them, he deals the blow on sin. Therefore, sin is no longer the problem between you and God but simply a misunderstanding of Jesus' mission. For instance, thirst is not a problem if water is available. But the availability of water does not solve the thirst problem until you actually drink the water. Or missing your way on the highway and making the wrong exit can land you in the wrong destination in the same way that missing Jesus "the way" can land you in the wrong spiritual destination. Jesus died for our sins, period. Nothing more nothing less. Hallelujah! Remember that you had to accept by faith that Jesus was crucified, shed His blood, died and resurrected to be saved or salvaged from the quagmire of sin, but not only sin but the inadequacies of the old covenant which never was a final solution to sin.

The old was mostly a materialistic covenant "based on the blood of bulls and goats." You had to be born a Jew to partake. Under the old, you could show material possessions as a sign of God's blessing. One could marry many women, take other people's land. You were even allowed to practice an eye for an eye.

But then scripture announces that'

"if there had been nothing wrong with that first covenant, no place would have been sought for another" (Hebrews 8:7).

Here's the crux of the matter: conventional wisdom states that the biggest problem facing the Church today is sin. The most persistent difficulty, the largest hindrance to living an overcoming life and the worst thing we have to deal with is sin. At least that's what we keep hearing. While sin must be addressed if we are to be in holy communion with the Lord God, I must respectfully disagree with the assumption that sin itself is the problem. Jesus has successfully dealt with the sin dilemma. He is the Lamb that *taketh away the sin of the world*! When he said, "it is finished" He meant *it is finished*. You need to believe it and the church needs to say AMEN, it is finished.

If the church will recognize, discern and live in the New Covenant, you will find that sin no longer wields outright power over us, Hallelujah! We are not as susceptible to sin as was the case when the laws of God were written on stone tablets as in the old. We now live by the law of the spirit. The gross misunderstanding of covenant and in particular, the new covenant, is the current hinderance. It is only under this covenant that you can "through the Spirit, mortify the deeds of the flesh;

"For if you live according to the flesh, you will die; but if by the Spirit you put to death the deeds of the body, you will live." (Romans 8:13 NIV)

You see, the old covenant did not have a permanent solution for sin; but the new covenant does. Many of our struggles as Christians really stem from a misunderstanding of what Jesus Christ actually came to do here on earth. The old covenant limited our access to God, but the new does not. Here is some exciting news: If we are walking in a right understanding of the new covenant and of what exactly Christ accomplished on the cross, then sin will not so easily ensnare us as we call on His Name. Hallelujah! This is Good News!

> "For the law of the Spirit of life in Christ Jesus hath made me free from the law of sin and death." (Romans 8:2)

This is why the scripture says, "Behold the

lamb of God that TAKETH [emphasis added] away the sin of the world" (John 1:29). The sin of the world was taken away two thousand years ago. Sin is no longer a problem but remains a plague to those who are not in covenant with the Lord by the blood of the lamb. It remains a plague to anyone who is not given totally to the New Covenant. We have the power now to resist and reject sinful desires and behaviors.

What Is Sin Anyway?

Sin really is a disruption of relationship. Sin is only a problem because it destroys relationships, while covenant produces real heartfelt and solemn commitment to one another. Take a look at the ten commandments. All the "Thou shall nots" are to protect a relationship. For instance, thou shall not kill is not there because God is afraid of being killed by humans. But because when you kill someone, someone else will suffer and may want you killed also. It creates chaos in the world. When you covet another's wife or belongings, I am sure her husband won't like you.

When you have other gods, it is outright disrespectful to the One who made you. He may not like you either. That's bad, right? Sin messes up marriages, breaks up families and destroys nations. Sin is usually rooted in deep seated selfishness. All the sinner thinks about is himself, at least at the moment of sin. When you make decisions, you must think about what you are agreeing to and if you can live up to it. Many think the best approach is to say what they have to say, do what they have to do for that moment and deal with the rest later. In fact many have said boldly to me and to others, "I will just repent later, but now I must do what I have to do." It is with this mindset that we approach God only to find out that "every idle word will be accounted for" and that God expects "your yes to be yes and no to be no" and that you reap what you sow. These are all under the new covenant because to whom much is given, much is expected.

Carnal people think of themselves first in everything. The spiritual ones focus on higher or spiritual things. They do not interpret life in terms of how it affects them first, but rather look at how the things that happen on the Earth affect God, others and themselves. It's a matter of focus, really.

The New Testament seems to me to have been written primarily for the spiritual. We hope and pray that the carnal will read it and experience a shift in vision. That shift is necessary if they are to understand and experience the life that the New Covenant brings. It is not for those who seek material things but for those who eagerly look for the King and His Kingdom. The New Testament runs counter to the carnal mind, for it is about self-denial, not self-indulgence. Its message is one of restraint in using the things of this world, for in this restraint lies the way to spiritual abundance.

The Scriptures are clear: We cannot be disciples of Christ unless we deny ourselves. We cannot continue to be enamored of the things of this world nor of our own ways.

"Let us strip off and throw aside every encumbrance (unnecessary weight) and that sin which so readily (deftly and cleverly) clings to and entangles us, and let us run with patient endurance and steady and active persistence the appointed course of race that is set before us. Looking away [from all that will distract] to Jesus, who is the Leader and Source of our faith [giving the first incentive for our belief] and is also its Finisher [bringing it to maturity and perfection]" *(*Hebrews 12:1b-2a, Amplified).

"Looking unto Jesus ["fixing our eyes," NASB] the author and finisher of our faith" (Hebrews 12:2a)

Let us focus on the Lord, seeking after Him and His ways. And let us learn to walk in the covenant He has provided—a covenant that frees us to know Him more fully as we walk in freedom in Christ.

God took you at your word when you committed your life to Him. For the one that will commit to Him after reading this book, you are making a decision to love and obey him at the same time. You agree to OBEY. You agree to make Him your only God. You agreed to shun sin.

Chapter Nine

But What About the Old

We have established the fact that the new covenant is superior to the old. We also know that we are no longer under the old covenant of Law, but we are God's new covenant people, bought with Christ's blood and sealed for redemption under the terms of the new covenant.

So what should we do with the old covenant? We should discard it. I don't mean the pages of the bible. Rather I mean the old covenant mindset. It simply is dangerous to mix the new and old.

" He also told them a parable: "No one tears a piece from a new garment and puts it on an old garment. If he does, he will tear the new, and the piece from the new will not match the old.   And no one puts new wine into old wineskins. If he does, the new wine will burst the skins and it will be spilled, and the skins will be destroyed. But new wine must be put into fresh wineskins. And no one after drinking old wine desires new, for he says, 'The old is good.'" Luke 5:39

You cannot mix the two. It never works. It is okay to be familiar with the old covenant but it is dangerous to live in it. It is even worse to try mixing the two. It would be difficult to understand or to appreciate the New Testament without first having a firm grasp of the old covenants that God cut with mankind in the past. Each of these covenants had its shortcomings; however, each found its fulfillment in the new covenant with the Blood of Jesus Christ.

The new covenant is like a drink of water to a thirsty person. This water is for those who hunger and thirst for righteousness because now they can be filled (Matthew 5:6). In other words, the old covenant created a thirst and an expectation; the new covenant fulfilled and satisfied this thirst and expectation.

The old covenant has historical value for us. It is for our learning and is recorded as an example for us (1 Corinthians 10:11). If we can look to the old agreements and understand God's dealings with man in that context, it will help us to better comprehend God's dealings with us under our covenant with Him. Looking to the Law of the old helps us to better appreciate the grace of the new.

We need look no further than the words of Christ Jesus or the writings of Paul to see the importance of the Old Testament Scriptures. Christ quoted from the old as He sought to bring people into the new. Paul often used the Scriptures in his writings as he contrasted old with new, thereby proving the new and showing its greatness as God's plan.

All believers should become familiar with the Word—the whole Word. It is often surprising when those who most adamantly declare the Bible to be the word of God admit that they don't read it often, or that they haven't even read the whole book. How can you know it is truth if you don't even know what it says? If we truly believe the scriptures to be God's word to us, then should we not be spending time in them to see what God has to say to us? If we are not familiar with the old, we will be denied the joy of seeing how the new fulfills and exceeds it. If you read with an open heart, allowing the Blessing of the new covenant—the Holy Spirit—to help you, you will soon find that there is not a single book in the Old Testament that does not point to the new. Where we sometimes fail is in spending so much time looking at the shadow that we ignore the reality. We must be balanced, approaching the scriptures with reverence. A very good example is found in the letter to the Corinthians where Paul explained Jesus from the old covenant. We read;

> **"Moreover, brethren, I would not that ye should be ignorant, how that all our fathers were under the cloud, and all passed through the sea; and were all baptized into Moses in the cloud and in the sea; and did all eat the same spiritual meat; and did all drink the same spiritual drink; for they drank of the spiritual Rock that followed them: _and that Rock was Christ_."**[emphasis added] (1 Corinthians 10:1-4)

"And that rock was Christ." That sheds the

whole light on the meaning of that rock episode and why that happened in the first place. The people to whom Paul wrote this letter had knowledge of the old. But they had only heard and read of these things as stories of the past. However, these events, as the apostle explains, point directly to Christ. Being familiar with the old covenant accounts, Paul's audience was able to relate to the new covenant teachings. Paul also wants us to learn from them, so he wrote;

"Now *these things were our examples*, to the intent _we_ should not lust after evil things, as they also lusted. Neither be ye idolaters neither let us commit fornication. *Neither let us tempt Christ, as some of them also tempted*, and were destroyed of serpents. Neither murmur ye, as some of them also murmured, and were destroyed of the destroyer. *Now all these things happened unto them for ensamples: and they are written for our admonition*, upon whom the ends of the world are come. Wherefore let him that thinketh he standeth take heed lest he fall."

But What About the Old

[emphasis added] *(1 Corinthians 10:5-12)*

Human history is really just made up of stories. It is a collection of many, many stories of people's lives, of the lives of nations and civilizations. We each have a story and it is largely up to us what that story will be. There are many stories of those who obeyed God and likewise many stories of those who did not. There are stories of overcomers, of people filled with faith and also of those who tempted God and murmured against Him.

In the scripture above Paul is reminding us of the exodus of the Hebrews from Egypt. He does not want us to forget what God did for His people. But he also doesn't want us to forget how those people responded. He reminds us of the sins that some of the people fell into and exhorts us to have nothing to do with these things. We may be walking in grace, but that does not mean we can do whatever we want. Sin is still sin. Yet we have the Blessing of the covenant to help us. We are no longer under compulsion to sin. We are free to walk in righteousness before God!

But What About the Old

"Then said he [Jesus] unto them, Therefore every scribe which is instructed unto the kingdom of heaven is like unto a man that is an householder, which bringeth forth out of his treasure things new and old." (Matthew 13:52)

It is true that we are among the sons of the new covenant, but we should not neglect or despise the lessons of the old covenant. We can learn much about the principles of Scripture and about God Himself by looking into the Old "Testament" Scriptures. They are the old treasures that point to the wondrous fulfillment Christ brought forth in the new. But the covenant itself is not for us.

Let's Be Careful

Jesus taught this concerning the old and new covenants:

"And he spake also a parable unto them; No man putteth a piece of a new garment upon an old; if otherwise, then

both the new maketh a rent, and the piece that was taken out of the new agreeth not with the old. And no man putteth new wine into old bottles; else the new wine will burst the bottles, and be spilled, and the bottles shall perish. But new wine must be put into new bottles; and both are preserved. *No man also having drunk old wine straightway desireth new: for he saith, The old is better."* (Luke 5:36-39)

There can be no doubt that here Jesus was referring to the old and new covenants. What is He saying? No one who is reasonable will take a piece of new cloth and sew it to the old. Why? The new piece will cause the old cloth to tear. Jesus is discouraging this because it simply is not a wise thing to do.

Obviously, Jesus is not speaking merely of cloth. He is saying that we cannot try to mix the Old Covenant with the New. This will only create confusion. How many believers do you know who try to sacrifice doves or oxen to the Lord? How many do you know who will not wear clothing of mixed weave? It seems kind of silly, doesn't it? Yet how many do you know who try to live their lives as believers caught up in legalism?

Legalism is what results when we try to mix the new with the old. Oh, we can try to mix the two. It may even seem to work for a while, but it will only work for so long before one of two things will happen: Either the rigidity of the old will choke the life out of the new (this is how modern-day Pharisees are made), or the new will burst forth from the old because it is too robust. It never worked together and it never will work.

We need to be praying in this hour that the Church will be able to break forth from the old to embrace the new. The old covenant religious forms cannot contain what God is doing and is about to do. The old style of leadership, the old legalism, even the old understandings of covenant and blessing and what it means to be a believer, will not be able to hold all that God is doing. The church should grow up.

So many preachers want to hold on to the old. Some do this out of ignorance while most preach

But What About the Old

a mixture of old and new because they want to take advantage of God's people. It's as simple as that. Doctrines like first fruits, wealth transfer, tithing, sowing seed and a host of other dubious teachings all come from the mixture of old and new. In fact, the whole prosperity error and false doctrine stem from the old covenant. It was only in the old that wealth was a sign of God's blessing. All the poster boys of financial prosperity / blessing doctrines are from the old. Abraham, Solomon and all of the stories come from the old. It was in the old that you could retaliate when wronged, the Jews will war and maim other nations with God's help. It was in the old that you could have several wives and even almost oppress women, kill a witch and kill homosexuals. In the old, one was a priest based on his family and place of origin.

We see why the old was limited and could not bring anyone to spiritual maturity. It was established by God to serve His purpose for the time and for the people and for the place for which it was established. It was not wrong for its intended purpose. The old was for children while the new is about maturing to the stature of Christ.

But What About the Old

It is wrong for us as Christian believers today to attempt to walk in the old. Why? Simply because it is the old. It has served its purpose, being our tutor until the new came. Now we have the new and it is Christ Jesus our Lord. In truth, Jesus is the new covenant. This covenant makes way for a better relationship with God. Christ is the;

"new and living way" (Hebrews 10:20).

Why would anyone put new wine into an old wineskin anyway, knowing that it would tear the vessel? Perhaps because people tend to be familiar and comfortable with the old? One might think the best way to cause them to accept the new is to put it into an old, familiar package. Yet;

"No man also having drunk old wine straightway desireth new: for he saith, 'The old is better.'"

We think that we are helping God by repackaging His message. But He isn't interested in gaining market share; He's interested in life and truth. The new is about abandonment of oneself to God and His purposes. It is for the mature. We have come of age in Christ. Let us stop chasing the old for its materialistic promises and give in to God.

Do you feel that something is being torn apart in your life? Can you feel a rumble in your spirit, the rumble of new wine fermenting, getting ready to burst forth in fullness? Then rejoice! Do not fear this kind of tearing, for it is simply the laying aside of the old so that the new may come forth. Yes, there is a tearing. Sometimes it may feel as though your spirit itself is being torn in two. Take it to the Lord. Ask Him to show you where you may be holding on to the old and how to lay hold of the new. Cast yourself on His mercy. There is no better place to be than in Him. The wineskin must be dealt with. The wineskin must be new again to hold the newness of the wine itself. The church must shed the old wineskin of activities and carnal control mechanisms. The church must toss away the old forms of temple-centered worship and start expressing God everywhere.

Chapter Ten

Discerning Old and New

The differences between the old and new covenants are many and most are fairly obvious when we read the Scriptures. But too often we fall into an old mindset. Paul exposes a major difference when he wrote that,

> **"Ye are manifestly declared to be the epistle of Christ ministered by us, written not with ink, but with the Spirit of the living God; not in tables of stone, but in fleshy tables of the heart."** *(*2 Corinthians 3:3)

Under the old covenant, the Laws of God were written on tablets of stone. They were handed down from on high, with the people of the congregation learning of the Law from their leaders. Under the new covenant, however, the laws of God are written on the tablets of our hearts. Even the newest believer has the Spirit within and the ability to hear and to heed what He is speaking. How many new Christians give up, of their own accord, sins with which they have struggled for years? Smokers turn away from cigarettes, the profane give up their foul language, even the ones that gossip cease gossiping. Why? Because they now have the laws of God written within their hearts. Their consciences, freshly laid bare to God, are convinced of the need to be better individuals. Desiring above all else to please their newfound Lord, they lay aside those things that would bring separation. Oh, that the Church would continually walk in such newness of life! Pray that the Lord would deal so once again with the Church and with your own heart.

> **"For the law having a shadow of good things to come, and not the very image of the things, can never with those sacrifices which they offered year by year continually make the comers thereunto perfect. For then would they not have ceased to be offered? because that the worshippers once purged**

should have had no more conscience of sins. But in those sacrifices there is a remembrance again made of sins every year. But this man [Jesus], after he had offered one sacrifice for sins for ever, sat down on the right hand of God; From henceforth expecting till his enemies be made his footstool. For by one offering he hath perfected for ever them that are sanctified." *(Hebrews 10:1-3, 12-14)*

No longer are animals sacrificed to atone for our sins. This form of sacrifice had to be given over and over; the blood of animals was not a complete atonement. But the Blood of Christ far surpasses that which had been offered. His atonement was offered once and for all people. Christ's Atonement need not ever be repeated, for it was perfect, full, complete and perpetually potent. It stands for all time, redeeming all who will come;

"Verily, verily, I say unto thee, Except a man be born again, he cannot see the kingdom of God." *(John 3:3)*

Discerning Old and New

Under the old covenant, a man had to be physically born into the tribe of Levi in order to become a priest. Only the Levites were able to minister before the Lord; and only one priest, once a year, was able to enter into the Most Holy Place. The people were relieved that this was so. They did not want to have to come face to face with the Lord God.

What a life-giving difference there is under the new covenant! First, as Jesus explained, it is not our physical birth that matters any longer, rather it is our spiritual birth. We needn't be born into a specific physical, natural family in order to become part of the family of God; instead, we must be spiritually born into God's family. Second, because the veil to the Holy of Holies was torn at the crucifixion, we have permanent access to God;

> **"Having therefore, brethren, boldness to enter into the holiest by the blood of Jesus, By a new and living way, which he hath consecrated for us, through the veil, that is to say, his flesh; And having an high priest over the house of God; Let**

**us draw near with a true heart in full
assurance of faith, having our hearts
sprinkled from an evil conscience, and
our bodies washed with pure water."
(Hebrews 10:19-22)**

Man has total access to God in the new. We
need wait for no other person to intercede for us,
for we have the great Mediator and Intercessor
who stands on our behalf saving us totally, our
Lord Jesus Christ;

**"Wherefore he is able also to save them
to the uttermost that come unto God by
him, seeing he ever liveth to make
intercession for them." (Hebrews 7:25)**

Ours is the awesome privilege of coming
before the throne not before a priest. This is the
blessing of relationship in the new covenant. For
how could true relationship be experienced in
fullness when there had to be an earthly
intermediary to mediate between God and man?
The sons of Israel had relationship with God, to be
sure—one need only read of David's experience
to see this. Yet this seemed to be the exception

rather than the rule. Did God not desire to enter into such intimate relationship then? I believe it is rather that under the old covenant man grew so used to seeking that intermediary, the priest, that he simply did not want to enter in, they wanted to maintain a distance.

But now we can grow in our relationship with the Lord, for He has rent the veil that once separated us, so that all may have that opportunity to enter in. It is a telling sign of the power of the old covenant mindset that the morning after the crucifixion, workers were reportedly set to work repairing the torn veil. We need not continue the repair, but may walk through with gratitude.

One of the most major innovations of the new covenant is the change in mindset. There is a scriptural principle that says;

"First the natural, and then the spiritual." (See 1 Corinthians 15:46.)

The old covenants, especially those cut with Abraham and David, were primarily materialistic in nature; except for the Messianic promises, they dealt principally with the natural realm.

But the blood covenant brings humanity to a new level of spiritual life and spiritual health. No longer are murder or adultery viewed as purely physical acts. Now, the righteousness the Lord brings extends to the life of the mind and the emotions as well. Our understanding is enlightened when we enter into this covenant. We are now being held to a higher level of accountability where not only our actions but also our thoughts are to be pure. (See Matthew 5:21-25; 27-30.)

The old covenant carried severe penalties for disobedience to the Law; the new covenant allows the grace of God to work as He lovingly disciplines His children. While His discipline can be severe, He also has empowered us to do right and avoid His wrath. We are spiritually more equipped under the New Covenant.

The ultimate divine intention is to put His laws in the hearts of all humanity,

"For this is the covenant that I will make with the house of Israel after those days, saith the Lord; I will put my laws into their mind, and write them in their hearts: and I will be to them a God, and they shall be to me a people: And they shall not teach every man his neighbour, and every man his brother, saying, Know the Lord: <u>for all shall know me,</u> from the least to the greatest. For I will be merciful to their unrighteousness, and their sins and their iniquities will I remember no more. In that he saith, A new covenant, he hath made the first old. Now that which decayeth and waxeth old is ready to vanish away." *(Hebrews 8:10-13)*

Church, the Scriptures themselves exhort us to remember who we are and of what covenant we are partakers. The writer of Hebrews vividly portrayed the two covenants;

"For ye are not come unto the mount that might be touched, and that burned with fire, nor unto blackness, and

darkness, and tempest, And the sound of a trumpet, and the voice of words; which voice they that heard entreated that the word should not be spoken to them any more: (For they could not endure that which was commanded, And if so much as a beast touch the mountain, it shall be stoned, or thrust through with a dart: And so terrible was the sight, that Moses said, I exceedingly fear and quake)." (Hebrews 12:18-21)

First he presents the old covenant. He paints the scene with a wide, dark brush, reminding the Jews of the fear that accompanied the giving of the Law. This passage is actually part of a longer section of exhortation, reminding these believers not to abandon their hope in Christ to return again to the Law. These people understood exactly what the writer was saying, for they had lived under the old covenant and knew its futility to bring them to peace with God.

After reminding his readers of this, the writer goes on to show the superiority of the new covenant in contrast to the old;

"But ye are come unto mount Sion, and to the city of the living God, the heavenly Jerusalem, and to an innumerable company of angels, to the general assembly and church of the firstborn, which are written in heaven, and to God the Judge of all, and to the spirits of just men made perfect, And to Jesus the mediator of the new covenant, and to the blood of sprinkling, that speaketh better things than that of Abel." *(*Hebrews 12:22-24)

We can almost see the sun breaking through the clouds as we read this passage! The new covenant is not about fear and guilt, but mercy and grace. The blood of Jesus really does speak better things.

Chapter Eleven

The Transitional Period

"For where a testament is, there must also of necessity be the death of the testator. For a testament is of force after men are dead: otherwise it is of no strength at all while the testator liveth. And almost all things are by the law purged with blood; and without shedding of blood is no remission." *(Hebrews 9:16-17, 22)*

According to this Scripture, the new covenant was not in effect until Jesus died, since *"without shedding of blood is no remission"* or forgiveness of sins. It was His Blood that ratified the new covenant which is why it is sometimes referred to as *"the new covenant, written in His Blood."* If this is true, then we can conclude that all that happened during Jesus' life on Earth took place during a transitional period. In fact, Jesus' life was

The Transitional Period

the transition. (Note that to speak of the New Testament experience, one is referring to the Christian experience after the cross. The time from Jesus' birth through the resurrection is a transition period.)

Therefore, many of the comments that Christ made to the people of His day, though valid, were not always directed towards Christians. When He answered certain questions, it was within the context of a Jewish/Gentile understanding. This does not reduce the power of His teachings in any way, nor does it by any means reduce their importance to the church. But His words and teachings must be seen in the light of a transitional period if we are to receive the full impact of what He was saying.

For instance, there were no Christian marriages until after Pentecost. When Jesus addressed issues of marriage, He was looking at a Jew married to a Jew, for that was the context of the question. However, when Paul taught about marriage many years later, there was a different kind of crisis. Now some believers were married to unbelievers; this was a different kind of situation.

This explains why the Pharisees were always around to challenge the teachings of Christ. In their estimation, Jesus' teachings were in direct conflict with the Torah. He was destroying the Law, the beliefs, and the practices of the Jews they thought. The Pharisees understood the Torah—at least, they were comfortable with their interpretation of it. This is very likely why Jesus did not provide very direct answers to some of their questions.

It was fairly obvious if one really listened to Him, that He was putting forth a different kind of thought, a new type of relationship between God and man. In the "Old Testament," God's blessing could be seen in the physical realm: wealth, property, animals, the blessing of God was measured in terms of material possessions, things that others could see.

Contrast this with Christ's teaching of what we call the Beatitudes:

"Blessed (happy, to be envied, and

spiritually prosperous—with life-joy and satisfaction in God's favor and salvation, *regardless of their outward conditions*) are the poor in spirit for theirs is the kingdom of heaven! Blessed and enviably happy [with a happiness produced by the experience of God's favor and especially conditioned by the revelation of His matchless grace] are those who mourn, for they shall be comforted!" *(*Matthew 5:3-4, Amplified) [emphasis added]

The amplified adds the words: "**regardless of their outward conditions**." That was exactly what the Lord was getting across. That is also what I am urging all believers to see. Jesus was offering a new understanding of what it means to be blessed. He continued to identify the blessed throughout this teaching—those who hunger and thirst for righteousness, the merciful, the pure in heart, the peacemakers, the persecuted. Jesus was teaching something new and different; no longer were people blessed because they were born into the right family—the Jews—now they were blessed based upon the condition of their hearts and spirits. The blessing was not in possessions, but in relationship with God. The heart condition determined if you were blessed in this economy.

If we are walking in the qualities of the blessed, then we are pure in heart. If we hunger and thirst for righteousness, if we are peacemakers, and all the rest, then we are light and salt. We are the blessed and the "useful to God." However, if we are not walking in these qualities, we have lost our light and saltiness. We cannot be light and salt in the world apart from having these qualities. Such are not blessed.

This teaching was so different from what had always been taught that Jesus knew it might be difficult for some of His listeners to grasp what He was saying. He also knew that some might not even want to grasp it. In fact, when Christ taught these things on the Mount, He must have surprised His listeners when He said;

"Think not that I am come to destroy the law, or the prophets: I am not come to destroy, but to fulfil." Matthew 5:17

The Transitional Period

Christ had been teaching about the blessed people, completing His teaching with the symbolism of light and salt, then suddenly He is talking about destroying the Law. What is this? His listeners must have shaken their heads at one another. What is He talking about? No one had verbally accused Him of any such thing yet, but he could see the body language and hear the baffled hearts questioning and disagreeing.

It was true. No one had accused Him of trying to destroy the Law or the prophets teaching. *Not yet.* But Jesus knew something that His audience that day did not. He knew that sooner or later the accusations would start flying around. His teaching was not a teaching that would endear Him to the Pharisaic Jews—or to any materialistic power grabbing person. Prior to Christ's coming, the Jews were always "favored": If there was any conflict, God was on the side of His people. But Jesus was telling them that the blessing was no longer simply a matter of physical birth; it had become a matter of being meek, and hungry, and thirsty, and poor in spirit. The blessing was being opened to all who would come. Jesus was making the covenant available to all. Everyone could be

The Transitional Period

favored by God.

There was "war" between Jesus and the teachers of the law. This war continued through the days of the apostles to the present day. But the Spirit of the word is here to impress the truth upon men's hearts. Carnality will lose its battle against the truth and the people will be set free.

Much of the Church today is caught up in an old covenant mindset. This is why there is such conflict in many areas and why the freedom and abundant life we read of in the Scriptures seem to be so elusive. This is why greedy prosperity preachers must rely heavily on the old. They have to because it would be very difficult to take advantage of people solely based on the new. The materialistic ingredients in the old covenant is dispatched regularly to put people in bondage.

There will always be tension between the old and new covenants because one is appealing to the spiritual and these two mindsets simply cannot coexist.

The Pharisees of Jesus' day realized that His

The Transitional Period

teachings were not just those of a good rabbi. They were revolutionary, for they were the words of one who breathed Spirit-given life into His listeners. Consider this passage from John chapter eight: There is an account that provides meaningful insight to the clash of covenants. It is not the only one but presents a good example. The story of the woman caught in adultery.

Two Mindsets Meet

We read as follows that;

"the scribes and Pharisees brought unto him a woman taken in adultery; and when they had set her in the midst, They said unto Him, Master, this woman was taken in adultery, in the very act. Now Moses in the law commanded us, that such should be stoned: but what sayest thou?" John 8:3-5

The woman's accusers stood ready to stone her. They knew the facts of the case. Under the old covenant Law, they had the right to kill her for her sin (although we notice that nothing was said of her partner). Now they had brought her to Jesus to hear what He would say. In other words, they were setting Him up. John observed that they were "testing" Him, looking for grounds for accusation (v. 6). Why did they do this? They understood that Jesus' teaching was in conflict with their old covenant understanding.

Under the old covenant, the Pharisees' actions would have been correct and consistent with Mosaic Law. But they did not want to prosecute the woman that day, nor did they want to execute her. The woman was not the issue. Instead, they wanted to incite a rebellion against the teachings of Jesus Christ. The old did not understand the new; therefore, it sought grounds on which to reject it.

Does that mean the old covenant was wrong? No, it was just not all that God had for His people. We would do well to keep in mind that Egypt was at first a place of *relief* for God's people. It only became a place of slavery and misery when they stayed there too long.

The Transitional Period

Jesus' ministry and teaching constituted a transitional period. The old was passing away, and He was proclaiming the new. Jesus' teachings often included phrases such as "Did you not read?" or "You have heard it said... But I say..." By this He was acknowledging that His listeners were familiar with the Old, but He would then go on to redefine what was actually being said. He was imparting a new covenant mindset to those who heard.

Our righteousness must exceed that of the Pharisees (Matthew 5:20); to whom much is given, much is expected (Luke 12:48). The new covenant entails greater responsibility because much is given to us. Think about the treasure of the Holy Spirit in you. This is by any standard the greatest gift possible. There was a time in history when the focus was on the action before the heart. But now God looks to the heart before the action. We sin in the heart even before we take an action.

It used to be that men's actions condemned them, but now it is the intent of the heart before the act. Defilement comes from within, not from outside contamination. God's Spirit dwells in us, and our thoughts are not hidden from Him. Sins that others cannot see must still be confronted, repented of, and dealt with in the light of God's forgiveness and mercy.

Chapter Twelve

Christ Is the New Covenant

From the time that God cut the first covenants with man, He knew that there would come a new covenant. The old covenants pointed toward this. From the Adamic covenant with its promise of One to come who would crush the serpent's head to the Davidic covenant with its promise of a King to reign forever, there has been a promise of Messiah. In Christ Jesus, that promise has been fulfilled.

God had planned the new covenant from the beginning, from before the beginning. For Christ truly is;

"the Lamb slain from the foundation of the world" (Revelation 13:8).

The day Jesus shed His blood at Calvary, the law was nailed to the cross. Jesus took our sins upon

Himself, even to the point of becoming sin;

> **"For he hath made him to be sin for us, who knew no sin; that we might be made the righteousness of God in Him." 2 Corinthians 5:21**

This shedding of Christ's blood was required for a full cleansing of sin. The blood of sacrificial animals was not enough to atone for our iniquities;

> **"And almost all things are by the law purged with blood; and without shedding of blood is no remission." Hebrews 9:22**

Why did it have to be Christ's blood that was shed? His is the only pure and sinless blood. No other person could have given this sacrifice for we are all tainted by sin. He also lived in this world with its contamination of sin. Jesus' blood does what no other blood could possibly do: Jesus has given us access to God continually. We may *"come boldly unto the throne of grace"* (Hebrews 4:16) based on the new covenant established by His

Christic Is the New Covenant

Blood.

It was at the cross that grace took over to complete what the Law could not finish. The purpose of the Law was to bring man to Christ, but the cross was necessary to complete that work;

"Wherefore the law was our schoolmaster to bring us unto Christ, that we might be justified by faith. But after that faith is come, we are no longer under a schoolmaster." Galatians 3:24-25

Paul taught that the old covenant was a schoolmaster, a tutor, whose task was to prepare man for the work of Christ;

"But before faith came, we were kept under the law, shut up unto the faith which should afterwards be revealed. Wherefore the law was our schoolmaster to bring us unto Christ, that we might be justified by faith. *But after that faith is come, we are no longer under a schoolmaster.* **For ye are all the children of God**

Christ Is the New Covenant

by faith in Christ Jesus. *For as many of you as have been baptized into Christ have put on Christ.* **There is neither Jew nor Greek, there is neither bond nor free, there is neither male nor female: for ye are all one in Christ Jesus. And if ye be Christ's, then are ye Abraham's seed, and heirs according to the promise."** *(*Galatians 3:23-29)

It seems that the Church today is like a young child who thinks that the other child's toys are better. Even though his parents remind him that what he has is better, still the child gazes longingly at his brother's toys. Only after the child matures, is he able to understand and appreciate what he has. Even so, we whine, and we fight, and we grasp until finally, somehow, maturity comes. Only with maturity can we really learn to appreciate what is ours. The Church is that younger child who is so fascinated with the old covenant material bounty. We are blind to the fact that our covenant is one of fulfillment of promise and of the true blessing. How long will we be content to gaze at the shadows when reality has been set before us?

Christ Is the New Covenant

The old covenant was a shadow of things to come. The time the prophets foretold is now. We are living in the time of the fulfillment of the Law and the Prophets! If you can lay hold of this, it will transform your life. It will transform the life of the Church, and it will transform the world. For too long the Church has plodded along, dutifully trying to lay hold of God's material promises to Abraham. We have been trying to walk in material prosperity by all means. Many have been using God's Word to justify and promote greed. We have spoken blessing and curses in the power of the promise to Abraham. But we are no longer living in the era of that shadow; we dwell in the light of the fulfillment in Christ! We can live in the blessing because the blessing is not material or physical. The blessing is not about the things you own. It is about the Holy Spirit living within you. It is about you becoming the temple of the Holy Spirit in truth. It is about God laying hold of you—and you of Him—and never letting go!

This was a mystery for ages past, but now God has brought revelation to His people. We read;

"But as it is written, Eye hath not seen, nor

ear heard, neither have entered into the heart of man, the things which God hath prepared for them that love him. But *God hath revealed them unto us* **by** *his Spirit*: **for the Spirit searcheth all things, yea, the deep things of God."** 1 Corinthians 2:9-10

How are your spiritual senses? Is your vision sharp to discern what God is placing before you? If not, then you have only to go before the Lord and ask Him to help you, for He gives wisdom to all who ask (James 1:5). Spending time in the Word and in communion with your Lord—not because you are "supposed to," but out of love—will help to hone your spiritual senses. Why is this so important? Because ours is not a covenant that may be carnally discerned. Words cannot fully explain what the Spirit perceives. However, we are not burdened by this, for we can be filled with His Spirit, Who leads and guides us to all truth. Eyes **had** not seen in the times of old, and carnal eyes still cannot see what God has revealed by His Spirit to us as the scripture says,

"But God hath revealed them unto us **by his Spirit."**

Christ Is the New Covenant

Under the old covenant, everything was spelled out. The law was written in stone, circumcision was physical and blessing was physical. But under the new covenant, everything must be spiritually discerned. True transformation is from this renewal. It is only by the Spirit of God that you may see the glory of our savior Jesus Christ. He has revealed all that we need to see if you are willing to see Jesus. This scripture does not speak of a future event but a reality you can own now. The greatest revelation of all eternity which is;

"the *mystery hidden for ages* **and generations but <u>now revealed to his saints</u>. To them God chose to make known how great among the Gentiles are <u>the riches of the glory of this mystery, which is Christ in you</u>, the hope of glory."** Colossians 1:26-7

To accept Jesus Christ is to accept the new covenant with God. The two cannot be separated. The transformation starts immediately before our eyes. Think of the newly born believers you have known; think back to how you were just after you were saved. Think of the overflowing life and exuberance, the joy and excitement at what God was doing. Jesus is the covenant; He is everything, He changes the heart and lying tongues have changed their ways, pride has become humility while the uncommitted have become committed. Miracles like these often happen when people come to the Lord simply because the desire of the heart has been changed by His Spirit.   The Lord has done what eyes had never seen nor had it entered the heart of man. The Law of God has been written deep in the heart and the soul is desiring more of God. The covenant was having its effect and the blessing becoming evident. The individual has now;

"Put on the new man, which is renewed in knowledge after the image of him that created him" *(Colossians 3:10).*

Jesus is the Key to our covenant. He brings the covenant and helps you fulfil your part. He truly is all we need. This is marvelous. It is all based on Him, secured by His sacrifice, and sealed by His Blood. So. let us put on the mind of Christ that we may see with spiritual eyes, discerning His will and desire for us. Our eyes have seen and experienced this great and glorious working of God in human existence.

Chapter Thirteen

The Better Covenant

The Book of 0Hebrews was written to Jewish believers to prove the superiority of Christ and His covenant. Such teaching had become necessary, since the Jewish believers who lived outside Israel were considering reverting to Judaism because of the persecution they were suffering. The Book of Hebrews was an exhortation and encouragement to these troubled, persecuted and disheartened believers.

The writer of Hebrews compares the priesthoods and the sacrifices. He shows that Christ is superior to the prophets and that His priesthood is superior to Aaron's. He is a Priest who serves in a better sanctuary and who offers a better Sacrifice. He is the Mediator of a **better** covenant that carries better promises. He is superior to the angels as well as to Moses. These things are all explained and delineated in the first seven chapters of Hebrews. Finally, the author says, "Now, this is the conclusion, the main point in all of this.";

> **"Now of the things which we have spoken this is the sum: We have such an high priest, who is set on the right hand of the throne of the Majesty in the heavens: a minister of the sanctuary, and of *the true tabernacle*, which the Lord pitched, and not man." Hebrews 8:1-2**

The tabernacle on earth was made by man's hand. The pattern was given by God, yet the building itself was merely a copy of the heavenly tabernacle. Our reality is in the spiritual realm. This is why Jesus did not offer any sacrifices as High Priest when He walked the earth. He had a **better** sanctuary and a **better** offering to make. His eyes were focused on the spiritual and your eyes should also be looking where the Lord is looking. We are living in better spiritual times. Jesus is;

> **"the mediator of a *better covenant*,**

The Better Covenant

[emphasis added] which was established upon better promises." Hebrews 8:6

We are all familiar with comparisons. If something is good, there is room for something better. The other covenants were good, but God had a better plan and a better covenant in mind. In a manner of speaking, He saved the best for last.

The new covenant is not just an extension of the old. It was totally new and infinitely better. Jesus likens it to new wine. Just as new wine had an inherent vigor that would tend to explode or destroy an older, more rigid wine container during the fermentation process, so the new covenant was totally new and had to be put within a new wineskin, a new form. The new covenant was robust—more radical teachings with more radical results in transformation. It was capable of changing men's hearts instantly and their perspective toward life. This was new wine! Don't settle for less.

Such potent and compelling approach is necessary because, walking with God is about His purposes, not our convenience. We must cling to our better covenant with better promises. When looking with carnal eyes, we will like what we see in the old. We like the land; we like the fact that those who curse us will be cursed and those who bless us will be blessed; we like the money; we like the status that all this will give us in this life and like many generations before us, we fail to see the spiritual connotation of all these things. Let us heed the words of Hebrews 11;

> "**These all died in faith, not having received the promises, but having seen them afar off, and were persuaded of them, and embraced them, and** *confessed that they were strangers and pilgrims on the earth. For they that say such things declare plainly that they seek a country*. **And truly, <u>if they had been mindful of that country from whence they came out, they might have had opportunity to have returned</u>. But** *now they desire a better country, that is, an heavenly: wherefore God is not ashamed to be called their God*: **for he hath prepared for them a city.**" Hebrews 11:13-16

The Better Covenant

The danger of turning back is always there if we keep looking back. We must keep looking forward and allow our eternal destination to consume our thoughts. The faithful Old Testament saints died knowing they had not received the promise. They perceived it. By faith, they saw it afar off with their spiritual eyes, and they longed for it. The ones that sought God received the revelation of the real prize. But the fullness of time had not yet arrived, and Christ had not yet come. Therefore, they could not enter into the promise. But we have entered into it and we live in it.

How can we abandon such a promise and seek to go back to an old covenant relationship? We have moved from Law into grace, from old into new, we have moved to sonship. We are to be true sons who love and honor their Father. Are you about your Father's business? Are you expanding His estate? We are to be caring for our Father's business, expanding His Kingdom. Like Jesus Christ, zeal for our Father's house should have consumed us by now. Like Him, our food should be to do the will of our Father. Obedience should be our source of sustenance, encouragement and motivation. If you are His child, you are filled with His Spirit. We can no longer claim ignorance of His ways because His Spirit, the Spirit of truth, has been given to us. He has been sent specifically to lead us and to guide us into all truth (John 16:13). This is part of our heritage in the new covenant. The first covenant was limited, but we have been brought to a new place now;

> **"For if that first covenant had been faultless, then should no place have been sought for the second. For finding fault with them, he saith, Behold, the days come, saith the Lord, when I will make a new covenant with the house of Israel and with the house of Judah: Not according to the covenant that I made with their fathers in the day when I took them by the hand to lead them out of the land of Egypt; because they continued not in my covenant, and I regarded them not, saith the Lord."**
> Hebrews 8:7-9

This day has come. God has made a new covenant with His people, and He has graciously extended that covenant to all who would enter into it. That day is now. Let us move forward and taste the spiritual flavor of the spiritual wine poured out for us as we commune in new and real fellowship with the Lord and with one another. This is a better covenant.

Chapter Fourteen

The Two Priesthoods

Just as there are old and new covenants, so are there old and new priesthoods. The first was the Aaronic priesthood, which God established through Moses. This was the priesthood of the Levites. It was set up to function in and through the Law. In fact, without the Law, there would have been very little reason to have established this priesthood, for much of the priests' daily work consisted of carrying out the Law, and of helping others to obey it.

Most believers are fairly familiar with the Levitical priesthood. We hear teachings about the Levites as we look at types and shadows in the Old Testament and as we look at patterns of worship. There are many crucial teachings to be found in looking at the Levites, and there are principles we would miss if not for the records found in the Scriptures concerning this special group of people. However, we are not of the Levites and pastors are not priests. Instead, every believer is a priest. Peter makes it clear when he was inspired by the Holy Spirit to say that;

"You also, as living stones, are being built up a spiritual house, a holy priesthood, to offer up spiritual sacrifices acceptable to God through Jesus Christ ... But you are a chosen generation, a royal priesthood, a holy nation, His own special people, that you may proclaim the praises of Him who called you out of darkness into His marvelous light" (1 Peter 2:5-9).

We do ourselves and our Lord a disservice if we limit what God is doing to the Levitical model. God is no longer operating in the same way He once did. When we see ourselves as priests, we will not live carelessly. However, when the "pastoral class" are seen as the priests, then most believers do not see the requirement to live a holy life style. They remain perpetual children that run to the "priest" for everything. The priesthood is a Holy one and that is what every believer is. We no longer need to make confessions to a professional priest but to one another if there is trust. We all are in the priestly service of our God. Our priestly calling comes from Jesus who was of a different priestly order unlike the Levites.

Jesus Vs Melchisedec

What is the history of Melchisedec? We have already seen the account as it is written in Genesis; the writer of Hebrews reiterates:

"For this Melchisedec, king of Salem, priest of the most high God, who met Abraham returning from the slaughter of the kings, and blessed him; To whom also Abraham gave a tenth part of all; first being by interpretation King of righteousness, and after that also King of Salem, which is, King of peace; Without father, without mother, without descent, having neither beginning of days, nor end of life; but made like unto the Son of God; abideth a priest continually." Hebrews 7:1-3

This is the extent of the biographical

information we have concerning Melchisedec. His face is shrouded to us, his earthly lineage unknown. While the Levites had to be able to trace their ancestral lines in order to minister, this man's lineage seems to be purposefully withheld from us. He springs, not from Law, but from Life. God Himself has set him in place to serve as a priest. But although we do not know much of this person, we do understand that he plays a pivotal role in the Scriptures. This king of righteousness and of peace is a forerunner of Christ. His priesthood is the one to which all will look to see the unending priesthood.

The Hebrews account continues, contrasting the two priesthoods;

> **"Now consider how great this man was, unto whom even the patriarch Abraham gave the tenth of the spoils. And verily they that are of the sons of Levi, who receive the office of the priesthood, have a commandment to take tithes of the people according to the law, that is, of their brethren, though they come out of the loins of**

Abraham: But he whose descent is not counted from them received tithes of Abraham, and blessed him that had the promises. And without all contradiction the less is blessed of the better. And here men that die receive tithes; but there he receiveth them, of whom it is witnessed that he liveth. And as I may so say, Levi also, who receiveth tithes, payed tithes in Abraham. For he was yet in the loins of his father, when Melchisedec met him." Hebrews 7:4-10

In other words, in Abraham the Levitical priesthood gave tithes to Melchisedec and received the blessing from him. Only after Christ came were the truths of this passage realized. Until that time, the Levites served as priests and the one to come after the order of Melchisedec had not yet been revealed. Once He had come, the surpassing nature of His priesthood was evident. Often this passage is used to justify tithing but clearly it simply was placing Jesus in the rightful place of superiority. I will not discuss tithing in this book. But I will state that Melchizedek blessed Abraham before he received tithe from him; Melchizedek, "met Abraham returning from the slaughter of the kings, and blessed him; To whom also Abraham gave a tenth part of all." So at the minimum, the two men did not see tithing as a source of blessing. This passage simply shows who was greater. Jesus is greater than Melchisedec;

> **"And without all contradiction the less is blessed of the better."** Hebrew 7:7

The Jewish Christians had real objections about the fact that Jesus was not a Levite. It was an intellectual disapproval but could keep them from maturity. Similarly, Christians can be held back by various issues that do not matter as much when it relates to Jesus and His saving grace. Jesus is the origin of our priesthood and the one we look to. Our natural pedigree has nothing to do with it but our spiritual pedigree. He is our example in all things. We read;

> **"Let us <u>look to the example of the One who has gone before us</u>, our Lord Jesus, who was a Priest "after the order of Melchisedec"** (Hebrews 7:17).

The Two Priesthoods

We have set our eyes on Jesus and will not lose focus. We do not look to fleshly commandments anymore. The fact that the priesthood had changed necessitated the recognition that there had to be a change in the Law also. Jesus brought radical change to everything on earth and for eternity. So, we read once more that;

"**If therefore perfection were by the Levitical priesthood, (for under it the people received the law,) what further need was there that another priest should rise after the order of Melchisedec**, and not be called after the order of Aaron*? For the priesthood being changed, there is made of necessity a change also of the law*. [emphasis added] For he of whom these things are spoken pertaineth to another tribe, of which no man gave attendance at the altar. For it is evident that our Lord sprang out of Juda; of which tribe Moses spake nothing concerning priesthood. And it is yet far more evident: for that after the similitude of Melchisedec there ariseth

another priest who is made, not after the law of a carnal commandment, **but after the power of an endless life. For he testifieth, Thou art a priest for ever after the order of Melchisedec.**" Hebrews 7:11-17

Notice that this is shown as a deliberate change. This was a permanent change that had taken place, and which would remain in effect. The new priesthood had actually made a change in the Law. This is because it does not spring forth from the Law because; *"the priesthood being changed, there is made of necessity a change also of the law.* [emphasis added] **For he of whom these things are spoken pertaineth to another tribe, of which no man gave attendance at the altar."**

"**For the law made nothing perfect, but the bringing in of a better hope did**; by the which we draw nigh unto God. And inasmuch as not without an oath he was made priest: (For those priests were made without an oath; but this with an oath by him that said unto him, The

Lord sware and will not repent, *Thou art a priest for ever after the order of Melchisedec:) By so much was Jesus made a surety of a better testament.* **And they truly were many priests, because they were not suffered to continue by reason of death: But this man, because he continueth ever, hath an unchangeable priesthood. Wherefore he is able also to save them to the uttermost that come unto God by him, seeing he ever liveth to make intercession for them.** *For such an high priest became us,* **who is holy, harmless, undefiled, separate from sinners, and made higher than the heavens."** Hebrews 7:19-26

The law made nothing perfect. Make a note of this because it remains a fact that the law showed weakness and unprofitability. What a blessing! Jesus actually intercedes for us all the time! He is exactly the one we need and we are an extension of Him because of His work on our behalf and inside of us by His Spirit. If we are to follow in this priesthood, we must also be people of prayer and intercession—pouring out mercy, compassion and healing upon others and their situations. We are to be those whose words are wisdom, knowledge, righteousness and truth, all bounded by love. Chapter seven of Hebrews ends with the affirmation that Christ our High Priest need not continually offer up sacrifices to the Father, as He gave Himself in atonement for us.

As the account continues into the following chapter, we are presented with Christ as He sits at the right hand of God, where He acts as our Priest. Here we see that just as there are natural (Levitical) and spiritual (order of Melchisedec) priesthoods, there are also natural and spiritual temples;

> **Now of the things which we have spoken this is the sum: We have such an high priest, who is set on the right hand of the throne of the Majesty in the heavens; A minister of the sanctuary, and of the true tabernacle, which the Lord pitched, and not man.**" Hebrews 8:1-2

The Two Priesthoods

This is an important distinction. Although the earthly tabernacle is patterned after the instructions given by God in the wilderness, it remains the tabernacle that was pitched by man. Our High Priest is not of that tabernacle, but of the true one; that is, the spiritual, which God has established. The earthly was simply a copy of the heavenly. While it was good and showed forth spiritual truths and was used as God desired, yet it was merely the shadow and not the reality. The real surpasses and overflows the earthly copy.

Interestingly, the writer comes back to the idea of the new covenant. This is central to all that he has written thus far. He establishes that every high priest is ordained to present gifts and sacrifices before the Lord. He also explains that Christ would not have been serving as a priest if He were still on the Earth; He could not do so according to the Law, since He was not of the tribe of the Levites. These earthly priests serve but the shadow and example. But what of Christ and His ministry? The Word has this to say concerning these things:

"But now hath he obtained a *more*

excellent ministry, **by how much also he is the mediator of** *a better covenant*, **which was established** *upon better promises*. **For if that first covenant had been faultless, then should no place have been sought for the second.** Hebrews 8:6

Finally, the Word sets forth what is perhaps the clearest articulation of the new covenant that we find in Scripture;

"For this is the covenant that I will make with the house of Israel after those days, saith the Lord; *I will put my laws into their mind, and write them in their hearts*: **and I will be to them a God, and they shall be to me a people: And they shall not teach every man his neighbour, and every man his brother, saying, Know the Lord: for all shall know me, from the least to the greatest. For I will be merciful to their unrighteousness, and their sins and their iniquities will I remember no more.** *In that he saith, A new covenant,*

The Two Priesthoods

he hath made the first old. Now that which __decayeth__ and __waxeth old__ is ready to __vanish away__." Hebrews 8:10-13

Now that the true High Priest has come, the old covenant with its old priesthood has been set aside. What does this mean in practical terms? It cannot be business as usual anymore.   It is not local church government in itself that is being addressed here. Rather, it is the old manner of doing things. We have a High Priest who is continually accessible, and who has continual communion with the Father—not one who may enter into the Holy of Holies only once a year. And we ourselves have continual access to the Father through Him, and through the veil that was ripped asunder. No longer is there a veil before us, separating us from the Holy of Holies, lest we enter in and experience the Presence of the Lord. Now we are invited to enter in and to come before the throne on our own behalf and on behalf of others.

No longer is it our works and the sacrifices we offer that make us acceptable in God's sight; it is the Sacrifice offered by our High Priest that has made us acceptable. It is not in the keeping of the Law and in the giving of offerings or the accumulation of good works that we find our righteousness. Jesus Himself has become our righteousness! This is the essence of the new covenant. It is not "Jesus and…" that brings life—not Jesus and my works, Jesus and my bible reading, not even Jesus and my prayers. Because we are now alive with the life of Christ, our appetites have changed; now we thirst for the word, we yearn for times of prayer, we seek to work righteousness. Life, blessing, peace, hope—all are through Jesus' blood alone.

Chapter Fifteen

The Two Tabernacles

"Then verily the first covenant had also ordinances of divine service, and a worldly sanctuary." Hebrews 9:1

"Ye also, as lively stones, are built up a <u>spiritual house</u>, an holy priesthood, to offer up <u>spiritual sacrifices</u>, acceptable to God by Jesus Christ." 1 Peter 2:5

God is Spirit, His worshippers, worship in Spirit and truth and He accepts spiritual sacrifices from His spiritual priesthood in His spiritual house.

The Church is the Body of Christ, the Bride. In this dispensation, things are different! *We do not have "ordinances of divine service, and a worldly sanctuary"*. Let me try this again; WE DO NOT HAVE A WORLDLY SANCTUARY! Again, we do not have a worldly sanctuary; *we* are the sanctuary! We are sacrifices holy and acceptable to God. Paul admonishes us with these words;

" **I appeal to you therefore, brothers, by the mercies of God, to present your bodies as _a living sacrifice_, holy and acceptable to God, which is your _spiritual worship_**" Romans 12:1 **ESV.**

Peter was also very clear in his explanation. He had to be—this was a new concept. The temple was no longer a building and man has direct access to God through Jesus. There was no sanctuary to go to. That is the profundity of the new covenant. The people of old were used to singing, "Come, let us go up to the mountain of the Lord," and "I rejoiced when I heard them say, 'Let us go to the house of the Lord.'" Everything worship was centered around the house of the Lord—the temple. But suddenly that journey was finished. Now, God lived within them. They didn't have to go to a specific place; wherever they chose to meet, that's where Church was. What a wonderful new truth! This explains why you will never come across any New Testament writer ever using language like "I went to church" or "James came back from church".

Many believers seem to think they are serving God if they visit a brick and mortar on Sunday. Many sadly feel like God is particularly impressed by this regular or occasional "visit." Furthermore, we advance this idea when we say words like "Sunday service." However, we are not necessarily serving or worshipping God just because we went somewhere on Sunday regardless of how many times we see the big signs on these structures saying "worship center," "Temple," Tabernacle," "Church," etc. We serve and worship God every day as every aspect of our lives is given over to Him for the service of the Kingdom. We serve God when we genuinely care about one another. We serve Him wherever we find ourselves. The primary objective of our corporate meetings is the coming together of believers who have been serving God all week. It is a time to be edified and refreshed by one another, renewing our love for one another in the Body of Christ. As the Spirit of the Lord draws us together, we can experience real fellowship with one another and with the Lord God. In reality, if we are the Church, then we cannot go to church; however, the Church can meet together in a building, at home or anywhere.

As though this weren't enough to cause confusion, we also hear mere men speak of "my church." Do we now own the Church? Of course not! Yet people's actions often support the idea that they do believe they own the Church, the very people of God. You would have heard these words before coming from a church leader: "my congregation," "my people," "my members," "my this," "my that." This may seem like a minor point; however, I believe it to be at the very heart of the new covenant misunderstanding. If the tabernacle of the new covenant is to be the "greater and more perfect tabernacle, not made with hands" (Hebrews 9:11), then man cannot own the new temple, which is God's people, His spiritual dwelling place.

The Building Is Blocking My View

The old covenant tabernacle stood as a reminder that the way into the Holy of Holies was not yet made manifest. The holy of holies is as close as we come to God. The closer to Him, the holier the place. It seems that too often our modern tabernacles have stood in the way of our seeing beyond and relating to God in that holiest of places. Again, we read;

"Priests go regularly into the first section, performing their ritual duties, but into the second section only the high priest can go, and he but once a year, and not without taking blood, which he offers for himself and for the unintentional sins of the people. *By this the Holy Spirit indicates that the way into the holy places is* <u>*not yet opened as long as the first section is still standing*</u> **(which is symbolic for the present age).** Hebrews 9: 6-9

Wow. These structures are truly blocking our view. The buildings command so much attention in maintenance and construction. We spend so much money and energy beautifying the worldly structure, which is not a sanctuary while the people suffer. But we usually get very little use out of this building. Most buildings are open only for a few hours on Sundays and a few more hours through the week. Sometimes believers are going through so much in their lives that they may need to spend extended time in the building praying, fasting or even resting. Yet too often this is not possible because we fear that our expensive equipment might be stolen. So, this space is frequently under lock and key, thereby denying free access to those who need it. The expensive sound systems and production quality equipment are priced more than human lives. The concert or theatre atmosphere must be maintained and the rehearsal for the next performance must go on. I remember a period in my life in a new city where I did not know many people. I was part of a small church group though. Yet I came close to being homeless and sleeping at a train station. No one in the group helped because I was expected to "use my faith" to overcome the circumstances or "sow my way out" of the situation. I was not even allowed to sleep in the building. Such foolishness is a result of bad teaching and faulty understanding of covenant. And yes, God did deliver me... from them. He will keep delivering me from such people although there is enough of them. These locations and these sometimes, overpriced constructions are simply wasted money. Recently, a group in an African country built "the biggest church building" that could seat thousands and thousands at once. A well-known pastor came to dedicate this building and had the nerve to refer to it as the "house of the Lord." These building projects are the greatest frauds performed upon the poor and rich alike. It is usually done to the weak-minded ones. Again, most believers today are weak-minded. Be wise and believe the word of God. The God we serve does not live in buildings constructed with the hands of men.

Many of these buildings are designed with a totally different function in mind: They are designed to accommodate more and more people as the empires grow. These monstrous constructions only feed the ego of the leader and require to be maintained like a beast. But where will these people find true community? Where did the term "mega church" come from? I am sure it did not come from the scriptures. Building size, crowd size, bank account size, private jet size and so on seems to be the measure of ministry success. What a shame.

Now please do not misunderstand the point

here. Christians do need a place to gather and fellowship. What is important though is the focus should be on the people of God. In other words, the time, the energy, the money—most of our resources—should be spent on the people of God first. Why should a believer who is in good standing within a local church body have to go to a bank for a loan if he has been making consistent contributions to the body? Let us make our investments in one another. The world will never respect us if we always come running to them for help. They need us, and we need to be mature examples of the Church for which Christ gave His blood. We must let that blood flow through our spiritual veins as we live out His call upon this earth.

We are the Church! No matter how lovely, how large, how wonderful our buildings are, God does not live in them. Let us begin to focus on the people of God. It is what we do for one another that matters in God's scheme of things. Paul declared himself to be a wise master builder at the end of his ministry (1 Corinthians 3:10), even though he did not build a single cathedral.

We now see that the Church is the people, not the building. There is something else we need to note here: *We are being built together into the dwelling of God*. Together. Not separately but...

Being Built Together

We must escape the, "It's just God and me" mentality. There are many reasons why people stay away from fellowshipping, but the "me and God" syndrome is the most outstanding reason. Much of it revolves around selfish behaviors. Self-centeredness is the reason why one can even be part of a local church, attending meetings every Sunday, and still not really be walking in fellowship with fellow believers.

If you want to be part of God's building, if you want to be part of the dwelling He is constructing in these days, then you must be built together with other lively stones. The only person who can do this kind of building is God. He does this through His ministry gifts. As you submit to Him and seek His will for your life, you will find that He will bring you together with a group of believers, and He will build you together with them. You will find your place. Peter wrote that we "as lively stones, are built up a spiritual house," and that;

"Ye are the temple of God, and that the Spirit of God dwelleth in you?"
1 Corinthians 3:16.

The word "ye" has a plurality attached to it here. "Ye" meant all of you together are being built. This letter would have been read to a whole church group. The New International version does a good job on this by asking the believers if they knew that;

" *__you yourselves__ are God's temple and that God's Spirit dwells __in your midst__?*

Obviously, one needs several stones to build a home- a spiritual dwelling for God. And yes, your body is the temple of the Holy Spirit but, no one individual can house God. God can only truly be seen as He is expressed through others and to others. God is community and He is building a community-a covenant community that reflects Him and His values.

The Two Tabarnalces

Where's the house we could build for the Lord God? There is none. Nothing we could build could ever contain Him. Yet the mystery and the glory of the new covenant is that God has chosen to dwell within His people. He is looking to the new Temple, the true Temple built without human hands. The writer of Hebrews in chapter nine compares the old and new sanctuaries and sacrifices.   Please patiently read the next scripture through. Don't read some of it but all of it, and pay attention to his conclusion. Again, consider seriously what he concludes that the Holy Ghost was saying through the standing physical temple structure. He writes,

"Then verily the first covenant had also ordinances of divine service, and a worldly sanctuary. For there was a tabernacle made; the first, wherein was the candlestick, and the table, and the shewbread; which is called the sanctuary. And after the second veil, the tabernacle which is called the Holiest of all; Which had the golden censer, and the ark of the covenant overlaid round about with gold, wherein was the

golden pot that had manna, and Aaron's rod that budded, and the tables of the covenant; And over it the cherubims of glory shadowing the mercy-seat. Now when these things were thus ordained, the priests went always into the first tabernacle, accomplishing the service of God. But into the second went the high priest alone once every year, not without blood, which he offered for himself, and for the errors of the people: *The Holy Ghost this signifying, that the way into the holiest of all was not yet made manifest, while as the first tabernacle was yet standing."* **[emphasis added] Hebrews 9:1-8**

Contrast this with the new covenant's sanctuary.

"But Christ being come an high priest of good things to come, *by a greater and more perfect tabernacle,* <u>**not made with hands**</u>**, that is to say,** *not of this building."* **Hebrews 9:11**

The new tabernacle is "not of this building";

the New American Standard translates this, "not of this creation." This tabernacle is created, not by man, but by God. It provides continual access to God which is the blessing of the new covenant. There is no hindrance, such as the old Tabernacle presented, to man's entering into the presence of God. No veils, no intermediaries, no animals to kill, no hurdles to jump.

During the time of the first Tabernacle, even the high priest never really entered into the holiest place. His was a physical approach rather than a spiritual one. It is only through Jesus and covered by His Blood that we can enter into the holiest place. I have said numerous times that the greatest gift you can give another person is access to you. This should come as no surprise because the first thing that happens when one person offends another is that access is denied to the offending party. This may be physical access, or it may be emotional access; either way, the result is the same. Fellowship has been cut off. Even in man's fallen state. Access is still everything. Politicians sell access to the president and important government officials. How much is access to God almighty worth? How much?

The Two Tabarnalces

Until the new covenant was ratified by the blood, before we drew near and received Christ, we were enemies of God. We lacked full access to Him. Oh, we had limited access; we could cry out to Him, for He always hears the cries of those who are drawing near to Him. Yet fullness of joy was not something we could experience before we came to Him. What does God desire in exchange for this access to Him? He wants access to us. The God of creation wants access to you. He wants full access to all areas of your heart and life. It is inescapable, He wants us to present ourselves as living sacrifices to Him; He wants us to carry Him about in us and with us. He wants to be the Treasure in your earthen vessels (2 Corinthians 4:7). And He wants to conform us to His image— the image of Christ.

After all, this is what being the Church is all about, carrying within us the very presence of God. Wonderful things happen when we give ourselves to this idea. When was the last time you raised someone from the dead? I mean someone who is dead in their trespasses, who has watched your life and listened to your words and gave their life to the Lord. When was the last time you saw a real miracle happen right where you were because you prayed for someone? Have you seen the complete turnaround in their life? Really, how many people have come to the Lord just because they have seen your lifestyle or listened to you? Do you know the gifts that God has placed in you? Wake up and see clearly. Humanity is lost and feeling their way through a confusing maze called life. Trying to figure out by themselves what this is all about and we have the answer. We possess the road map and can direct them to the Lord. To the real holy of holies where they can spiritually fellowship in close communion with the Lord that created them. Can you feel the call?

Chapter Sixteen

Entering Into the New Covenant

What is the message of the gospel? God wants you back. He wants to be in a close covenant relationship with you today. It is that simple...it is that transforming. God wants you back from living for just yourself to living for Him in covenant with others. He made you and He loves you, and He wants to transform your life. The Lord wants you to agree with Him and come home. The Bible reveals that God was in Christ reconciling the world to Himself and He has now given us the ministry of reconciliation. Which means in turn that Christ is in us reconciling the world to Himself. How marvelous. Read this for yourself in the bible;

"In Christ God was reconciling the world to himself, **not counting their trespasses against them, and entrusting to us the message of reconciliation.   Therefore,**

we are ambassadors for Christ, *God making his appeal through us.* **We implore you on behalf of Christ, be reconciled to God." 2 Corinthians 5:19-20 ESV**

Perhaps you are one of those who are content to live day to day, week to week, year to year without relating to God. Perhaps you are one who doesn't take the time to pray, to read the Word, to worship. Or perhaps you are one whose heart is continually reaching out to the Lord, whose thoughts are as prayers, who counts the moments until you are free to worship, to hear His word, to bask in His presence. We need to be in fellowship with God, in communion with Him continually. Our lives are to be a praise and a prayer unto the Lord.

God loves us and has made Himself available to us. Return to Him for He has given Himself for us and to us. The greatest gift that God could possibly have given us is Himself and His Presence; therefore, the only reasonable gesture is to give Him yourself. After all, you did not make yourself in the first place, but you cannot give Him anything less. Yes, He wants you and you will do well to listen to this appeal. Therefore, the greatest punishment that God can inflict upon us is to withdraw that holy Presence from us. This is why the Scriptures show us that Jesus is the Bread of Life, the Way, the Truth, the Life, the Word, the Light. He has been made wisdom and revelation to us—He is everything that we need. His presence is as necessary to us as the air we breathe. May He never distance Himself from us. It is time to return because things are practically winding down. The age is on a fast track towards ending. The world as we know it will be destroyed. Yes, it will. Be wise and discern the times.

The Sign of Jonah

Do not become like the ones who are so entertainment-oriented that they always want a sign. Some physical, dramatic or miraculous sign as a herald of God's plans. We read the following verses with sobriety.

"The Pharisees also with the Sadducees came, and tempting desired him that he would shew them a sign

> from heaven. He answered and said unto them, When it is evening, ye say, It will be fair weather: for the sky is red. And in the morning, It will be foul weather to day: for the sky is red and lowering. O ye hypocrites, ye can discern the face of the sky; but can ye not discern the signs of the times? *A wicked and adulterous generation seeketh after a sign;* and <u>there shall no sign be given unto it</u>, *but the sign of the prophet Jonas.* And he left them, and departed." Matthew 16:1-4

The Pharisees and the Sadducees apparently had a knack for reading the sky. This was how they could forecast the weather. But when it came to the things of God, they were not so adept. Their spiritual radar was dull. So they came to Jesus, asking Him to show them a sign from Heaven. Their carnal perspective affected them and everyone they taught, influencing the understanding of most of the Jews of the day. Like today many run from end to end, church to church, prophet to prophet. "Show us something, perform something even if it is fake." Jesus said that the **sign** will be the **sign of Jonah**. This sign has been given and understood by the spiritually minded. *Just as Jonah became a sign to the Ninevites, so will the Son of Man be to this generation.* **Jonah's** restoration after three days inside the great fish prefigures His own resurrection. Again, we read;

> **"The men of Nineveh will stand up at the judgment with this generation and condemn it, for they repented at the preaching of Jonah; and now something greater than Jonah is here. Luke 11:32 NIV**

Jesus is resurrected and getting ready to come back in glory. Do not become one of those who will experience His judgment. See to it that the men of Nineveh will not be pointing at you on that day. This will happen. It is not a fairy tale. Be warned. Ninevites will say "Wow, we didn't even have the information, resources and benefit of hindsight, yet we repented." This will be a shame, right?

He will come back for His church, His covenant people who are waiting for Him. The ones that are committed to Him and to one another. This is true because you cannot love God if you don't love your brother whom you see. His covenant people will not be condemned with this or any generation. Glory to God. You must be chasing after Him and not signs, and miracles, and nice sounding words that lack power to deliver your soul.

So how are we to enter into the new covenant? Very simply, by faith in Jesus. Confessing Him as our Lord and Savior. We must ask the Lord to renew our minds. We must allow ourselves to be transformed, laying our spirits open to receive the new covenant, sealed by Christ's Blood. We must read the Word, asking the Holy Spirit, our teacher and guide, to open our minds and hearts to understand what He would say to us. We must be aware of satan's schemes and resist the ever-present pull of materialism, as well as other sins and desires that would separate us from our God. We must go forth as the priesthood and the Bride that we are, showing forth God's glory.

Jesus is the Way, and He will guide you by His Spirit until you come back to Him. He is the Door that opens to you, taking you into a new vista of eternal joy. He is the Bishop of "heaven's cathedral" in the presence of our Father. Listen to what the Lord is saying, and remain focused on Him. Learn to hear His Voice, that you may not be swayed from His ways.

The new covenant is for you. It is an agreement between God...and you. God desires that you walk in the reality and knowledge of the Blessing He has given. The fullness of the Spirit is a gift and a blessing that He has for you.

May you enter into the Blessing of the new covenant!

Please say the following prayer:

Heavenly Father, I confess that Jesus is now my Lord and I believe that you, God raised Him from the dead. Please forgive me of all my sins and fill me with your Spirit. Thank you for accepting me in the beloved and making me a covenant child of yours. Amen.

ABOUT THE AUTHOR

A truly gifted teacher, speaker and author, Upjohn Aghaji has made important contributions to the body of Christ through his insightful teachings. He breaks the bible down into very simple and understandable terms. He has lived and worked as a fine artist in the United States for almost 30 years with his wife and children. Pastor Upjohn has led some church planting and mission efforts in and outside Africa.

This is the author's second book. His first is titled, *Discover Your Hidden Blessing*. He has also written several articles that can be read on the Inspire Ministry International, Facebook page. These include, "God's Time Is the Best Time," "You Are the One We're Waiting For," "True Believers Should Stop Saying These Now," "Christianity Is Not About Money, Never Was and Never Will Be" and more.

Through reading The Hidden Covenant, your understanding will be open to what it really means to be in covenant with God.

www.ingramcontent.com/pod-product-compliance
Lightning Source LLC
LaVergne TN
LVHW011157080426

835508LV00007B/465